Succeed Naturally, the *I Ching* Way

Succeed Naturally, the *I Ching* Way

Unraveling the Wisdom of Natural Laws

Lily Chung, PhD

Author of *The Path to Good Fortune*

iUniverse, Inc.

New York   Lincoln   Shanghai

Succeed Naturally, the *I Ching* Way
Unraveling the Wisdom of Natural Laws

iUniverse books may be ordered through booksellers or by contacting:

iUniverse
2021 Pine Lake Road, Suite 100
Lincoln, NE 68512
www.iuniverse.com
1-800-Authors (1-800-288-4677)

Because of the dynamic nature of the Internet, any Web addresses or links contained in this book may have changed since publication and may no longer be valid.

The views expressed in this work are solely those of the author and do not necessarily reflect the views of the publisher, and the publisher hereby disclaims any responsibility for them.

ISBN: 978-0-595-47805-7 (pbk)
ISBN: 978-0-595-71495-7 (cloth)

Printed in the United States of America

Contents

Chapter 1

Introduction

Goal of the Book

In 2003, our world entered a metaphysical cycle of bursting innovations and chaotic competition. The trend will continue for twenty years. Young men are leading, setting rules, innovating on all fronts, and contending for bigger shares of socioeconomic goods. These galloping contenders are constantly breaking and making rules. Quick actions dominate our social scene.

We are in constant turmoil as a few big winners pop up in our social landscape from time to time while the majority of us live in despair and fear. The gaps between the haves and have-nots and between the successful and the unsuccessful are widening at an accelerating pace. It is confusing and frightening. Handling our bottled-up anger and fear before they ignite into a roaring disaster requires great wisdom.

Are there laws to govern a seemingly lawless state? We break or revise man-made rules in response to our changing circumstances as soon as we create them. We need natural laws.

Those who succeed in this world abide by natural laws and move with the natural flow. A lucky few were born to embrace natural laws without knowing it. Some have learned how to do so haphazardly; many are unaware of the power of natural laws.

What are Natural Laws?

Natural laws are the laws that exist in nature and maintain the order of cosmic reality. This reality reflects the interaction of the cosmic flow, the physical environment, and the human response. They are the laws of the king of the cosmos.

To get some idea of how natural laws work, imagine how the planets move in their orbits: all move constantly in one direction and within one orbit. Natural laws are entirely impartial and immutable. Other examples are the shift of the four seasons and the rotation of day and night. Many natural laws are implanted in the human mind and regularly followed without the least understanding of them.

The discipline of physics is definitely the best study of natural laws. Being close to nature keeps us inspired by the natural order of things. In addition, history teaches us great lessons, including how dynasties flourished and died in a natural course. Philosophers dedicated to delivering the truth about the total reality of time and space have unfolded some codes of natural laws.

Why Do We Need Natural Laws?

We live in a reality that involves the interplay of a cosmic force called flow. In fact, cosmic flow is by far the most decisive force shaping our global, physical, and social landscapes. History proves that significant discoveries, victories, and disasters are the results of natural forces. People succeed suddenly at the onset of the right cosmic flow. These claims are fully and strongly supported by my extensive research over the last twenty years.

Some of my research on this regard was discussed in my publications listed in the reference but most of it, by far, was discussed in my workshops to students in Europe, Canada, California and in some cruise tours which included audience worldwide. However, the most dramatic examples on the effects of cosmic flows on humans are found in the marital life of celebrities. I have published a book on "The Truth of Relationship, Why People marry and divorce?" It covers the marital history of 15 celebrities in the western world, including presidents and movie stars.

The publication essentially explains how cosmic flows bond individuals and accounts why and how people married and divorced as a result. Since it was written in Chinese, it is not listed in the reference. Most of the content was, however, shared with students in my workshops (conducted in English) in Canada and California.

Without the help of the right cosmic flow, we can work very hard but remain in an endless struggle, moving around in life with little progress. Sadly but truly, cosmic flow divides humans into distinct categories from birth. This mystery is stubbornly holding up.

One or two sages in China discovered the nature and cycle of cosmic flow thousands of years ago at about the time when the *I Ching* was written. The possible name of the sage(s) and the process of discovery was discussed in length in "The Path to Good Fortune" listed in the reference. This led to the development of the Chinese lunar calendar, an ancient guide for Chinese farmers and a basic tool for all Chinese divination systems. Sorting out the impact of cosmic flow to on human destiny and how its rules work on individuals was, however, a slow process. The first formal divination system, known as the four-pillar system, was completed in the ninth century.

The four-pillar system can map out the cosmic energy field of an individual and its path of periodic changes over the person's lifetime. This cosmic energy field determines the endowments and life path of the individual. The map will help the person find the right career, spouse, and residence by spotting and capitalizing on energy peaks and being cautious during low cycles. The system is fully elaborated in my previous publication *The Path to Good Fortune: The Meng*.

Just as we have to obey the will of God, we cannot change the path of the cosmic flow. Though everyone fills a niche predetermined by the Almighty and his plan, we all have free will to choose how to fulfill our roles. That is, the options on how to sail through our journeys are wide open. Our attitude, knowledge, and skill in that matter determine the nature and magnitude of our success and define the outcome of our efforts.

The strategy boils down to picking the right options. The right option is one that is naturally correct, meets the approval of the cosmic king—the Almighty—and is compatible with the natural laws.

Great inventors such as Isaac Newton and Thomas Edison, Nobel Prize winners, and Olympic gold medalists all scored victories during one of the peaks in their personal cosmic energy cycles. The story on the apple and the laws of gravity might be legendary but Newton's discovery was truly a product of the surge of wood flow in his cosmic cycle; the onset of wood energy (such as an apple or an apple tree) was, in fact, his key to success. As a metaphysician on Chinese divination, I have elaborate, unpublished research data to support this claim. As a co-incidence, Thomas Edison also owed his victories to wood flow in his life path. I have the document of research as well.

The procedure of mapping out our cosmic energy composition and its cycle of change is explained the "The Path to Good Fortune." It might sound mysterious but it is well documented and well applied worldwide to the knowledgeable, mostly Chinese.

Highly perceptive individuals worldwide have been troubled by this cosmic reality. Plato commented that "Nature's judgment is always final." (P.40, The Story of Philosophy). Isaac Newton was avidly engrossed in finding natural laws in the Bible. Thomas Edison commented: "Nature is not merciful and loving, but wholly merciless, indifferent." In other words, no one can bend natural laws. (religion and metaphysics in the "Life of Thomas Edison").

Albert Einstein summed up this very disturbing new discovery as follows" There is no place in physics for the field and matter, for the field is the only reality." (P 2, The Cosmic Energy Web).

The cosmic reality is beyond the accountability of the physical laws derived from the sciences. This order, known in modern physics as quantum mechanics, has puzzled physicists since the twelfth century. Cosmic flows and natural laws have remained popular but debated topics among intellectuals worldwide.

To function properly in this cosmic reality as an inseparable unit, we need to play by its rules by obeying natural laws. Where can we find a complete set of natural laws in society to guide us on day-to-day issues in this fast-changing global community? For convenience and efficiency, we need such laws packed in one handy document, categorized by functional themes, to meet our specific needs.

Natural Laws in the *I Ching*

Knowledgeable scholars from across the globe agree that the *I Ching* is the best, most complete source of natural laws. The *I Ching* recognized the cosmic reality (the only reality, in Einstein's words) long before any other documented sources. It has laws to account for this ultimate reality, the total cosmic reality extending beyond all physical, scientific accountability.

Its natural laws are packaged into sixty-four functional categories, each in the form of a hexagram, covering practically all sociopolitical topics of our society from leadership and management to behavior. Each hexagram is a little thesis, including principles, strategies, or procedures to address specific issues. This collection of natural laws is the authentic and ultimate value of the *I Ching*.

Unfortunately, the *I Ching* has been pervasively presented and used as a divination tool. *I Ching* scholars worldwide have spent more time arguing about the interpretation of passages than delivering the proper messages. In self-defense, many scholars include a few interpretations of individual passages but hesitate to deliver conclusions.

The *I Ching* was written at a time when written language was in its initial, primitive form; usable words were sparse, and each had to be painstakingly constructed with a rope or crafted with a manual tool. To effectively address the complexity of the issues included in the cosmic reality, its writer or writers adopted a seemingly simple but mysteriously profound approach.

First, the writer or writers invented a marvelously concise symbol system, collectively known as the *Ba Qua* (the eight trigrams), as a description tool.

Second, they deliberately used the names of tools, utensils, plants, and animals in society as analogies to supplement the symbols in delivering messages. Because the utensils and most plants and animals no longer exist to give clues about the passages today, unraveling the symbol system requires metaphysical knowledge. The *I Ching*, therefore, remains one of the least understood books.

Most readers are unable to see the whole picture of the hexagrams. Very few can see the natural laws among the commentaries. Over the history of the *I Ching*, only two exceptional minds could penetrate its backbone and present its natural laws in two authoritative documents.

The first person was Lao-tzu, a globally renowned metaphysician born in northeast China, in probably 570 B. C. according to the research of some modern historians. As he lived an obscure life and his work was not recognized by his contemporaries, it was impossible to determine his birth time. In any event, he was definitely born after I Ching was written.

Lao Tzu which means "old scholar" in Chinese, was probably a convenient name created for this mysterious legendary sage. His only published work, *Tao Te Ching (Laws on Gaining Power from the Tao)*, discusses the codes of natural laws, or the *Tao*, in eighty-one modules.

His book contains simplified versions of the *I Ching* laws in plain, ancient language without symbols. It filters over the passages and completely reorganizes the *I Ching* laws to address eighty-one different themes.

Being the first person to present natural laws by categories, he was considered the first physicist in China long after his death. His *Tao Te Ching* was translated into many languages (second after the Bible) in the twentieth century, making him a well-known philosopher worldwide. While many people have benefited from the wisdom of these natural laws, hardly anyone is aware of the authentic origin of this wisdom. Readers who are familiar with the laws in both Tao Te Ching and the I Ching would agree with my comment.

Tao Te Ching does not package the laws of the *I Ching* in a hexagram by individual themes. The laws are completely reorganized to serve different functions and to illustrate how physical and social forces work in general. In other words, there is no strategy or procedure regarding a specific issue for the public to follow, as illustrated in the *I Ching*.

The second document is a divination system invented by Kan-Tze Shaw (AD 1011–1077), the greatest and most respected Chinese metaphysician whose name, sadly, has never traveled beyond China or been translated into any languages other than Chinese. Using mysteriously intuitive but powerful mathematical formulas, he precisely converted the complete *I Ching* commentaries, line by line, into a divination system. Each original commentary has turned into a verse of a poem carrying an enticing message. Fundamentally, the system carries the force of natural laws to the ultimate level of cosmic reality beyond the comprehension of the ordinary population.

The divination system, with its poems that forecast events with amazing accuracy, is considered the most functional and the most respected among all Chinese divination systems. It is the most well-known but least practiced, as very few people know how to use it.

This book is listed in our reference documents.

The Message of this Book

The previously mentioned authoritative books demonstrate the mysterious, versatile power of the *I Ching* laws, one on the social and political fronts and the other in the metaphysical domain. The *I Ching* laws serve both the social reality and the cosmic reality. The I Ching has guided countless individuals. Two top minds, a physicist and metaphysician, owed their success to its laws. This truly marvelous book should be made easy to understand so ordinary people can benefit from its teachings.

The *Tao Te Ching* is only understood by a small number of sophisticated intellectuals, not the larger population. It also does not deliver the complete *I Ching* laws. The divination system, due to its complexity, is even more difficult to understand.

How can the general public share the power of the *I Ching* laws and benefit from its wisdom? We need to clear a few roadblocks. One longstanding roadblock is the inconclusive interpretation of the *I Ching* passages among its various published forms. This irresponsible attitude, both pervasive and popular, encourages fruitless divination and creates confusion about the truth of the *I Ching*.

My book aims to change that mentality. I address each hexagram with the foolproof rules of the symbol system and arrive at consistent conclusions. Each conclusion is presented in simple, straightforward language.

The fundamental roadblock is the *I Ching* symbol system, which includes the *Ba Qua* and the yin and yang lines. No publication properly illustrates the symbols. Without good knowledge of these symbols, no one can understand or benefit from the *I Ching*. My breakthrough book addresses this issue with elaborate examples.

Knowing the rules of these symbols not only helps us properly interpret the *I Ching* passages but also protects us from the confusion of illusive interpretations. We can read the *I Ching* with confidence.

These rules serve an additional purpose. Although I have tried hard to preserve the original meaning of the *I Ching* passages while delivering the laws, my book can never be perfect. For an original document on the laws of the *I Ching*, a reliable base for evaluating the accuracy of the interpretation must exist. These rules on the symbols provide an objective yardstick.

Structure of the Book

I devote two chapters to the symbol system of the *I Ching*. I discuss the nature and interaction of the five elements, the yin and yang forces, and the rules for reading a hexagram.

I will guide readers through the proper procedures for reading the laws of the *I Ching* by discussing fifteen of the sixty-four hexagrams. Although the themes of all sixty-four hexagrams are timeless and universal, the selected hexagrams are more functional and relevant to our modern daily needs.

I have organized the fifteen selected hexagrams into four themes:

- Achieving fame, leadership, and wealth
- Managing relationships
- Managing adversity
- Enriching personal development

I illustrate each hexagram and examine its attributes, line structure, and line commentaries. Direct translations of the original line commentaries are in italic type, and my comments follow. I offer elaborate instructions for interpreting each of the fifteen hexagrams. Readers should gain sufficient insight and skill to explore other *I Ching* hexagrams on their own.

The remaining hexagrams are illustrated and summarized in the appendices. Readers interested in learning more about the natural laws in the *I Ching* can refer to the appropriate hexagram for guidance and divination.

Chapter 2

How to Read the *I Ching*

The origin of the *I Ching* has remained a mystery explored by hundreds of scholars over thousands of years. I don't believe unraveling the mystery is necessary. I can't imagine such a pool of marvelous cosmic truth coming from a single human mind. It has to be a gift from God.

Scholars agree that the *I Ching* is a collection of operating laws for the cosmos. It is likely a book on "natural laws" and a guide for how governments and individuals should make decisions. How do we prove this?

There is a golden rule among experts on the *I Ching*: "Those who understand the *I Ching* do not divine." The *I Ching* is about cosmic truth, natural laws. When we abide by natural laws, we make "naturally correct" decisions. To be naturally correct all the time, we need to learn the laws thoroughly. As natural laws become part of the fabric in our lives and grow with us, we can readily predict the outcome of an event. There is no need to divine.

Its Symbol System

The *I Ching* speaks of the five components, or elements, of the cosmic forces. It identifies two fundamental, opposite forces known as the yin and the yang. All things interact, competing and empowering one another. Simple examples of yin and yang are husband and wife, risk and gain, day and night, and the seasons.

Yin and yang forces contrast in nature. They compete with but also complement the other. For example, a husband and wife work together when the relationship is managed in proper order, enriching both lives. They may also spar on critical issues. The interaction makes each person grow in the process.

Taking risk can bring us gain or loss. Gaining seemingly makes us happy, but it can also make us complacent; losing might be unpleasant, but it can put us on the winning edge for the next battle. Day and night rotate, taking turns dominating the cosmos; each is equally crucial to the harmony of nature.

Selling and buying are yin and yang forces. From the point of the seller, the seller is the yin force and the buyer is the yang force. The competing interests are selling at maximum profit versus buying at lowest cost.

If the seller only focuses on making the highest profit without considering the needs and the financial capacity of his buyer, his strategy may be "all yin and no yang." He does not interact with the other force; he can never sell, and the buyer does not get to buy. To succeed, yin and yang have to strike common ground, a fair price and profit for both parties. This is the essence of the *Tao*, seemingly simple but comprehensively compelling and profound.

Successfully balancing the yin and the yang—requires a functional strategy and a good knowledge of the *Tao*. Each hexagram in the *I Ching* is a separate thesis of the *Tao*, laying a strategy for striking.

The hexagram starts with two lines: a solid line (_____) is the yang force, and the divided line (__ __) is the yin. Three lines make a trigram. A trigram is the fundamental building block of the hexagrams. Each trigram manifests a wide range of attributes (see figure 1). I will explain the function of these attributes later in this chapter.

There are eight trigrams. Altogether, they represent the complete cosmic order in eight cardinal directions. The eight trigrams and their attributes define the fundamental nature, order, and function of each dimension of the cosmos. This is why nosy people in China are nicknamed "Eight Trigrams" or referred to simply as "Eight."

Figure 1 is the first comprehensive display of attributes for the eight trigrams. The significance of such attributes has never been discussed in a systematic manner in any *I Ching* publication, a breakthrough.

Trigrams

Using figure 1, let us explore how these attributes work. In the column of social order, the trigrams represent a family of eight: father, mother, three sons, and three daughters, always in this order.

In the column of moral attributes, the traditional five Chinese virtues are represented by all trigrams. A father has to be fair (the nature of metal) and wise, someone having a good mind; a mother has to be reliable and forgiving (the nature of the earth), having a wide abdomen to tolerate and care for others; the oldest sibling must be kind and caring; and the middle son, squeezed in between, needs wisdom to move around. The middle daughter, as a female, needs a different strategy: she must practice courtesy to avoid confrontations. The youngest siblings devotedly follow the leadership of the elders.

Each family member symbolizes a time of day and a season. The father, as the head of the household, is in charge of food storage and distribution; he represents late fall (when harvest is complete) and late evening (when security measures are taken to protect family members. The mother, in charge of domestic matters, symbolizes the evening (the dinner hour) and late summer (when the harvest is packaged).

	Chien	Kun	Chen	Sun	Kan	Li	Ken	Tui
	6	2	3	4	1	9	8	7
Form	☰	☷	☳	☴	☵	☲	☶	☱
Element	Metal	Earth	Wood	Wood	Water	Fire	Earth	Metal
Nature	Heaven	Land	Thunder	Wind	Rain	Sun	Hill	Pond
Social Order	Father	Mother	1st son	1st daughter	2nd son	2nd daughter	3rd son	3rd daughter
Body Part	Head	Abdomen	Foot	Hip	Ear	Eyes	Hand	Mouth
Direction	NW	SW	E	SE	N	S	NE	W
Season	Winter	Late Summer	Spring	Early Summer	Winter	Summer	Late winter	Fall
Animal	Horse	Ox	Dragon	Rooster	Pig	Bird	Dog	Goat
Hour	9+PM	4+PM	6+AM	10+AM	11+PM	Noon	2+AM	7+PM

Figure 1: Trigrams and Attributes

Hexagrams

A hexagram consists of an upper and a lower trigram, forming six lines. Each of the eight trigrams doubles up with every other trigram, creating sixty-four hexagrams. Each hexagram represents a thesis on one operational law of the universe, expressing an idea, concept, reality, procedure, or ethical strategy.

Each line in the hexagram is called a *yao*. The lines are numbered from bottom to top in ascending order.

A nine precedes each number for a yang (solid) line, and a six precedes each number of a yin (broken) line. This is shown in figure 2. Line one is a yang line; it is referred to as "Nine 1." Line two, also a yang line, is "Nine 2." Line four, a yin line, is "Six 4."

Outer or Upper Trigram	Nine 6	━━━━━	Top, risky, nonfunctional
Foreign Territory	Nine 5	━━━━━	Middle, highest function, king
Lines 4, 5, and 6	Six 4	━━ ━━	Peripheral, shaky chief assistant
Inner or Lower Trigram	Nine 3	━━━━━	Peripheral, risky
Home Front	Nine 2	━━━━━	Middle, protected fortunate
Lines 1, 2, and 3	Nine 1	━━━━━	Humble position

Figure 2: The Hexagram of the *I Ching*

The logic? Nine is a powerful number, while six is a weak number. This ancient Chinese idea is shared by Western numerology. It has fascinated modern physicists who claim that the cosmos was created in ten stages. Planning occurred during the first half of the creation. Building started at stage six; the cosmos was in its weakest form, the typical nature of a yin force. Stage nine indicated completion; the cosmos was in its most powerful form, the typical nature of a yang force. Perfection of the cosmos occurred during stage ten.

Because many people find the system confusing, most English publications on the *I Ching* use a simple system of one to six, regardless of the nature of the line. I will follow this simplified system with all hexagrams in this book. To read a hexagram, you must understand its four parts: its position and structure of the lines, the numeric order, the line commentary, and the alternate trigrams.

Position

All odd-numbered lines denote yang positions, and all even-numbered lines denote yin positions. It is fortunate for a yang (solid) line to fall in a yang position (lines one, three, and five) and for a yin (broken) line to fall in a yin position (lines two, four, and six). Such correctly positioned lines are said to fall in the natural order. A male performs the duty of a father, and a female, the duty of a mother. It results in natural harmony and therefore carries good fortune.

Being in the right position guarantees legitimacy, entitlement, and, eventually, success. It ensures smooth sailing. Because a line denotes the condition or outcome of an event, it carries a message in divination about a positive move or a desirable breakthrough. The person in such a line is in his or her right mind, doing the right thing, and is entitled to stay in that position.

When a yang line falls in a yin position, or vice versa, it is out of its natural place, which naturally creates unfortunate outcomes. An individual may have the wrong career, have the wrong mate, or be in an awkward circumstance (such as being at a casual-dress party in a ball gown). Being in the wrong place creates frustration, unhappiness, and misfortune; the magnitude of the distress depends on the circumstance.

In figure 2, lines one, three, and five are in the correct yang positions. Line four, a yin line, is also properly positioned. These lines create good fortune. Lines two and six are in the wrong positions; they are yang lines placed in even-numbered, or yin, positions.

When your life cycle happens to fall in an incorrect position, you have to proceed with caution and allow yourself more space to adjust to mishaps. Chances are that you will have to fight harder and settle for less. The odds are against you.

Lines in corresponding positions in both the upper and lower trigrams form a bonding team. For instance, the middle lines in both trigrams, lines two and five, are bonding lines. Other corresponding teams are lines one and four and lines three and six. Corresponding lines of opposite genders create good fortune; there is a bond between them. Bonding pairs can count on support from each other. Each of the lines has a bonding mate, which gives each some security and protection. These pairs of lines are bonded for mutual support.

Corresponding lines of the same gender (both yang or both yin) are not desirable; there is no bond between the mates, and the partners are not supportive of each other. Under these circumstances, we need to be highly alert and cautious in anything we do because we cannot count on a partner for support. We want to keep a low profile. Harmony and bonding are essential ingredients for natural success and happiness.

As shown in figure 2, lines one and four, yin and yang respectively, make a good supporting pair. Each has a bonding mate, a fortunate situation. The other two pairs do not have bonding mates.

Numeric Order

Each line carries a social order. Line five, a king position, commands the highest social honor. At the middle of the trigram, it is well sheltered from both ends and, therefore, well protected. Being protected is a favorable natural order; you are blessed.

In divination (the system invented by Kan-Tze Shaw discussed in Chapter 1), people whose birth cycles fall on line five normally occupy high positions (they are usually leaders in their fields), having progressed easily from a secure base; this guarantees a good life. Both Princess Diana and Jacqueline Kennedy Onassis had their life cycle falling into line five.

This most preferred position, being high, also ensures room to move upward i.e. to line six), if desired. Many Chinese emperors who inherited the throne had a life on line five.

Line two, the corresponding partner of line five, is the second-best position. It enjoys great opportunities, favoritism, and naturally easy success. At the middle of the lower trigram, it is also protected. Lines two and five are the most desirable positions in anything we do. They represent the key lines in any hexagram.

Both lines two and five are centered at the middle of the trigram, meaning they are balanced in the energy field, possess proper perspectives, and are in the right frame of mind to make correct decisions.

Line four comes third in the social order. Being right next to the king, it is the chief assistant, most trusted, and likely to advance to high positions. It is, however, in a shaky position for two reasons: First, it is most likely to take the king's rage and to be punished. Second, it is at the outer edge of the trigram and open to attacks. For people whose birth cycles fall on line four, opportunities abound, but achievements come from hard work, and life is uncertain. President Richard Nixon's life fell into line four.

Line three is also a risky position, as it is on the upper edge of the lower trigram, exposed to dangers and attacks. The person is, however, in a good position to enjoy new opportunities, move to a new city or country, and ultimately succeed, but only under favorable circumstances. This line lies in a transitional zone with changes on the horizon. That is why the Chinese use the saying "not three not four" to express uncertainty.

Line one is a humble, undefined position indicating an unpredictable course. No one can predict how a humble person will turn out in the long run. A humble person could be forever a little guy or forced to achieve greatness in unexpected circumstances. It is the position of new beginnings.

Line six, the peak position, is unique. It represents a critical moment in life demanding one's full attention. Unfortunately, because it is on the top, the only way to move is downward. This is the core of the *I Ching* wisdom. People in such a position are likely to have a volatile life, coping with big surprises or losses. They certainly will have more than their share of excitement.

Wise people will try by all means to avoid reaching the sixth stage of any development because they don't want to fall. Chinese emperors were nicknamed "His Majesty of Nine 5." They chose a yang (Nine) line for its power. From line five, the highest line within the safe zone, one can move upward or sideways without worrying about falling. One of the most important reasons for learning the *I Ching* is to be able to identify the critical top stage, the breaking point, or the end of a development and avoid it.

There is one exception. A sage or a great leader should have no problem staying on the top, and he forever remains at line six. This is the mystery of the *Tao*. Even an infallible law allows exceptions.

Does line position always affect a person's reality? It holds up quite well. In my practice, a person whose life chart occupies line two or five has a good chance of becoming the boss or taking a position of leadership and is more likely to stay in his or her position for a long period of time; but such a person is not necessarily a high achiever. His or her high position comes easily.

Lines three and four are the most likely positions for high achievers. Great presidents occupied line four and founding fathers held lines three or six; they are the risk takers. The founder of Yuen and Ming dynasties (in China) occupied line six.

Line Commentary

Each line in the hexagram carries a commentary indicating the principle involved and an action or strategy to be used at a given point. The commentaries of each line can convene a theme among the six lines. They can also represent an independent scenario, offering a separate perspective of a theme. As a rule, the line commentaries are concise and, at times, illusory. Reading the line commentary takes some expertise.

We take into consideration the following elements when reading the line commentaries: the form of the line, its position, and the corresponding line. The five elements and the interaction of the yin and the yang forces have to be put into proper perspective. The commentaries are to be understood in the framework of time and space.

Alternate Trigrams

We can derive four trigrams within a hexagram. The two at each end (formed by lines one, two, and three at the bottom and by lines four, five, and six at the top) are the fundamental trigrams. These trigrams carry the primary message of the hexagram.

In between, three consecutive lines (lines two, three, and four and lines three, four, and five) also form a trigram. These two intermediate trigrams are called alternate trigrams, as shown in the example below. Alternate trigrams contribute messages of a secondary nature for the hexagram.

All trigrams deliver the theme of the hexagram. To interpret the message of the hexagram, follow this procedure:

- Identify each of the trigrams.
- List the attributes of each trigram, using figure 1.
- Construct a scenario from the attributes.

I'll use the forty-fifth hexagram, *Hsui* (Clustering), to illustrate the procedure. *Hsui* is about attaining a good life by accumulating resources. Having too many resources or assets creates confusion and other unwanted consequences. *Hsui* speaks about using discretion to trim unnecessary wealth.

To derive the messages from this hexagram, let us first outline the four trigrams: *Kun* and *Tui*, the fundamental trigrams, and *Kan* and *Sun*, the alternate trigrams.

For each trigram, we copy the attributes from figure 1. They are listed below the trigrams. Let us establish the scenario from these attributes.

```
————  ———— 6

————————— 5

————————— 4

————  ———— 3

————  ———— 2

————  ———— 1
```

Fundamental Trigrams   **Alternate Trigrams**

```
3 ——  ——    6 ——  ——    4 —————    5 —————
2 ——  ——    5 —————    3 ——  ——    4 —————
1 ——  ——    4 —————    2 ——  ——    3 ——  ——
```

      Kun   *Tui*   *Kan*   *Sun*

Kun: earth, mother abdomen, integrity, southwest, late summer, and ox

Tui: metal, pond, young daughter, mouth, justice west, fall, and goat

Kan: earth, hill, young son, integrity, northeast, late winter, and dog

Sun: wood, wind, first daughter, hip, kindness, southeast, early summer, and rooster

First, let's examine the natural scene. Both *Kun* (earth) and *Kan* (mountain, highland) provide the fields of different elevations for various crops. *Sun* (wood, plants) and *Tui* (pond or water in a regulated pool, ready for irrigation) supply the seedlings and water for cultivation. The field is fertile with abundant, growing plants producing bountiful crops.

The people involved with the land are a mother, two daughters, and a son. The women tend the farm with the children's help. The time is early afternoon and evening, a busy time for cooking. The season is late spring to early fall, a time for cultivating the harvest, a working season.

People are working on fertile land during working and producing hours. The result is the accumulation of assets. Wealth comes from hard work and teamwork.

The trigrams represent several body parts: the abdomen, hip, hand, and mouth. The mouth is on the top, the outer territory. A person whose life cycle contains this hexagram is likely to be a great communicator, using the mouth to make a living. This person sits and writes as well. There are four yin lines and two yang lines; the greater number of yin lines represents this person's tendency to do mental work. With yin lines at both ends, in the outer territories, this person is courteous and flexible and mixes well with the public.

Chapter 3

Rules on Reading a Hexagram

The theme of each hexagram in the *I Ching* expresses a part of the *Tao* (the operating laws of the universe). The *Tao* is the totality on the exchange of two fundamental components: the five elements and the bipolar forces of yin and yang. Their interaction creates all lives and things and is responsible for all happenings in the universe.

Understanding the interplay of the five elements and the yin and yang forces is essential to grasping the theme of each hexagram. No book can cover all phases of the interaction. No one has ever tried to write such a comprehensive book because no one will succeed. I'll try to cover some fundamentals to help my readers.

The Five Elements and the Laws of Life

The universe, as the Chinese sages perceived it, is a space composed of five elements: wood, fire, metal, water, and earth. Each element has its domain: wood/east, fire/south, metal/west, water/north, and earth/center. This order is true to the geography of China.

The elements take turns ruling the universe. Wood reigns in the spring when vegetation thrives; it is visible and takes in plenty of water, hollowing the earth. As summer approaches, fire takes its turn. The sun is bright, the heat is strong, and the days get longer. Metal matures in the fall. It becomes solid and shiny, perfect for turning into great tools. Water rules in the winter and threatens fire, soaks up the earth, uproots trees, and undermines metal.

In the ending month of each season, the dominant element wanes in power, leaving a gap for the earth to fill. Earth dominates the months of March, June, September, and December in the lunar calendar, which are approximately April, July, October, and January in the Western calendar.

The five elements interact and are responsible for all energy flows and all forms of life in the universe. There are numerous interactions, but two are most important: interbreeding and inter-ruling.

To breed is to support or empower. Water breeds wood; it supports the growth of wood, thus producing more wood. Wood breeds fire by fueling it. Fire breeds earth by providing warmth to keep organisms in the ground alive, which creates living, productive, powerful soil. Earth provides a home for all metal, so earth breeds metal. Without earth, no metal can grow. Metal breeds water. The cycle repeats.

To rule is to control. Wood rules earth, as it can penetrate into the soft soil. Earth controls water by absorbing or blocking it. Water extinguishes fire, and fire melts metal. Metal tools chop down wood.

In theory, every element has an equal opportunity to breed and to rule. The strength of each, however, varies with time, space, and its interaction with the other elements. The interaction of the elements becomes the base of all cosmic energy flows. Each year, month, day, and hour is dominated by the interacting flows of some of the five elements.

How do the theories of the five elements apply to the laws of life? All things, living and nonliving, are products of the five elements. All our blessings are governed by the five elements. Due to the different structures of the five elements in our systems, these elements mean different things to different people.

Since each element has its own domain and takes its turn dominating the cosmos, only one or two elements thrive within the universe at any given time. For example, when water rules, wood could be empowered and thrive too. When metal rules, water becomes empowered as well.

Life is filled with change, as the title *I Ching*, which translates to "Book of Change," implies. No one should, therefore, expect to passionately love another person forever or to enjoy wealth as much as when it was first acquired. Everyone should always be ready for changes and adapt to them. Learning the laws of change will ensure a smooth path.

In the *I Ching*, each trigram represents one of the five elements. As two trigrams combine to make a hexagram, the elements interact and deliver a message. I will touch upon these interactions as we read the hexagrams. I hope readers will grasp the essence of the discussions and apply the ideas to the other hexagrams and eventually to the happenings in their own lives.

The flows and the energy exchanges among them were discovered by a legendary Chinese sage, Fu Hsi, long before the *I Ching* was written. The exact time of the discovery was impossible to determine as written language was barely in use for record keeping. They are registered in the perpetual lunar calendars by year, month, and day. The lunar calendar was the guide for Chinese farmers to schedule their farming operations.

It has also become the basic divination tool for all Chinese metaphysicians. Serious readers of the *I Ching* use the lunar calendar when they divine from the hexagrams. An English conversion of the lunar calendars, together with the reading instructions, can be found in my 1997 book, *The Path to Good Fortune.*

In the *I Ching*, the five elements also denote the nature of a cardinal direction, the social rank of a person, the timing of an action, or a social virtue, as indicated in the chart for the eight trigrams in chapter two. This is best illustrated with a hexagram.

Dating咸 31

Fundamental Trigrams   **Alternate Trigrams**

Ken   *Tui*   *Sun*   *Chien*

By referring to the chart in chapter 2, we can identify the elements in the fundamental trigrams: earth and metal. Earth nurtures metal, and metal loosens or enlightens the earth when the earth gets too thick; this is known as an "inter-supporting" relationship. Dating is fundamentally a mutually supportive endeavor. Partners in the process should support each other.

The alternate trigrams contain a secondary message. Their elements are, respectively, wood and metal, indicating an inter-ruling relationship. Successful dating takes more than supportive partners. A competition for control occurs between the partners. Competition is fundamental in human nature.

One must tactfully control his or her emotions for self protection and for a favorable outcome. Support for one's partner has to be supplemented by good self-control to avoid overindulgence. However, support is fundamental, while competition is secondary.

The social value for *Ken*, an earth trigram, is integrity, and for *Tui*, justice. Integrity and fairness are complementary, like earth and metal. On the alternate trigram, the elements are represented as kindness and fairness. Justice is about fair play, leaving very little room for kindness. Yet, the emotion involved in dating requires leniency mixed with control.

Which virtue stands out in the dating process? Justice, or fair play, takes up half of the trigram group. But what about strength?

Consider the time and the direction of the trigrams. The time is mainly fall, the non-producing season after the harvest, when metal is most powerful. Wood and earth are both weak, as the trigrams indicate. Metal, therefore, stands out as the dominant element governing the act of dating. This means we need to date the right partner to begin with and behave fairly and properly. Improper, strong emotions between the wrong partners create misfortune.

There are additional messages in the structure of the yin and yang lines in the hexagrams. We'll return to these trigrams after a discussion of yin and yang forces.

Yin and Yang Forces

The yin and yang forces contrast in nature and function. Yet, they complement each other by maintaining the check-and-balance state of the universe.

Yang is the expression of all masculine things. Examples include males, the sun, daytime, summer, odd numbers, and bright colors. In nature, yang is forward going and virile. This force is more powerful than yin.

Yin, of the feminine gender, is the expression of retreat, docility, gentleness, slowness, smoothness, and submissiveness. Examples of yin forces are females, the moon, nighttime, winter, even numbers, and most subtle and dark colors. Regardless of their lesser physical power, they contend equally with or are even more destructive than yang forces, depending on the circumstances.

As a rule, in normal situations, yin and yang coexist. Whatever we do, we face a competing force, either yin or yang, such as the self-interest of another person. Failing to perceive the other force is inviting trouble.

We might jeopardize our health or social relationships by pushing our ambitions too far. A tyrant (a yang force) might encounter revolution (a yin force) from suppressed subjects when his or her control goes unchecked. Bosses who always put their profits above the benefit of their employees will not stay in business for too long; people who always want to grab the last dollar end up losing big.

Studies have consistently shown that people who act on one force fail eventually. A study by two professors at Knox College in Illinois on a thousand adults from thirteen countries showed that people who value extrinsic goals are more prone to behavioral problems and physical ailments. The gold diggers scored far lower on measures of vitality and self-actualization. They were also more likely to abuse drugs, alcohol, and cigarettes. An article in *Forbes* magazine on April 5, 1999, popularized this study (article:" Poor me, I'm rich in reference).

The study illustrates an "all yin and no yang" scenario. A person who sees only the good things money can do and goes after it single-mindedly is acting on all yin (or internal) forces. Neglecting the negative consequences of wealth is dangerous.

Bob Lutz, retired chairman of Chrysler Corporation, shared his business philosophy in the book *Guts (article: The Vintage Contrarian)*. One of his seven business laws claims: "Companies that do make lots of money tend to be run by the enthusiasts who, in the normal course of gratifying their own tastes and curiosities, come up with products or services that so excite their customers that those companies end up making lots of money." This is another example of yin and yang interactions.

The enthusiasts, in "gratifying their curiosities," were indeed influenced by yin and yang interactions while making and testing hypotheses. Their products and services happened to be the perfect children of the yin and yang, meeting the needs of both buyers and sellers. Excitement from a company's customers pours money into its pockets.

Yin and yang also take turns reigning the cosmos, as seen in the rotation of sunrise and sunset and the change of seasons. People, and even countries, go through ups and downs (yang and yin cycles). Winners and losers might reverse course in due time. To survive, we employ different forces to meet the demands of our circumstances. Knowing the rules and using the right forces at the right time can make us winners.

Yin and Yang Rules in the *I Ching*

The *I Ching* offers the best and the most complete information about the interplay of the yin and the yang. Symbols represent the forces. A solid line denotes the yang force, and a divided line represents the yin. Except for the first two hexagrams, a combination of solid and divided lines illustrates how yin and yang forces work together to deliver a message.

Chien, the first hexagram in the *I Ching*, is the only all-yang hexagram; it illustrates the nature of yang forces. *Kun*, the second hexagram, explains the nature of the yin force with only yin lines. The consequence of using only one force is almost always unfortunate; at worst, it can lead to isolation, stagnation, or loss. The commentaries in the sixth line of each hexagram carry more serious, disastrous messages.

Metaphysicians in *feng shui* design avoid using all-yang or all-yin elements by all means. As a rule, they try hard to balance the opposing forces. However, there are exceptional circumstances that occasionally call for only one force to be employed. People who may use one force to accomplish a goal are martyrs, spies, selfish dictators, or lifetime dependents (such as those who are physically or mentally disabled). But such people pay a high price to achieve their goals or get what they need.

The golden rule in the yin/yang interplay is about "non-contending." The best scenario is equilibrium of the opposing forces, meaning both parties are committed to promoting mutual benefit and are equally happy. The result is great success.

The *I Ching* has only one hexagram providing laws to this great fortune. It is number sixty-three, Success, which appears below.

Success 63

Fundamental trigrams   **Alternate trigrams**

The two fundamental trigrams are water and fire, inter-ruling elements representing conflicting yin and yang interests. No one can succeed alone. Success involves the assistance of other people. Conflicting interests must be put to mutual benefit.

Water can extinguish fire, but it has reason to keep fire alive to make its life more valuable or comfortable. Fire can dry up water, but it can also enhance its value. How do we create the equilibrium of these two conflicting elements?

Both parties must be committed to promoting mutual benefits. Water, by nature, stays below the surface, and fire rises above the ground. However, in the hexagram, these trigrams reverse positions; each tries to bend the other way for mutual benefit. Water needs fire, and fire is ready to help. We may need to sacrifice some comfort (yin) and to acquire some skill (yang) to succeed. We need to balance productive and counterproductive attitudes and make the effort to change destructive habits.

Yin and yang lines are in equal numbers and positioned correctly (yang lines in odd positions and yin lines in even positions) in the hexagram. Both parties stand on level ground in the proper positions and are committed to fair play. They must switch to the right force as needed.

In the line structure, every yin line appears above a yang line. While two parties are rarely in equal strength to begin with, the stronger party is advised to make slight concessions to the disadvantaged by putting its interests slightly ahead to accomplish a goal.

Every pair of lines represents corresponding teammates. Each party has the interests of its counterpart in mind all the way, and both work together to iron out conflicts. The four trigrams in the hexagram are in equal numbers of water and fire, alternately positioned, reinforcing the ideas of cooperation and fairness.

The top line of the hexagram is a yin line representing the environment (or external forces); the bottom line is yang line representing the self. To succeed, we need to remain confident, persistent, and flexible, modifying our strategy based on results. In other words, we need different attitudes in different circumstances.

While yin and yang forces influence success, more factors are involved. The hexagram contains body-part symbols showing the importance of the eye and the ear, which diligently collect and absorb data. We must employ the virtues of great knowledge and wisdom (shown in the repeating water trigrams) and demonstrate plenty of courtesy (shown in the repeating fire trigrams).

Below is another not-so-perfect example of the balance of yin and yang forces.

Dating 31咸

All yin lines stay outside, while all yang lines stay inside. Dating is an emotional experience; one has to be open, gentle, observant, and flexible on all fronts while preserving integrity and keeping commitments to the other party.

Courtship is about bonding. All pairs of lines remain bonded; however, lines one and four are not in the proper positions, just as logic and judgment are never perfect when emotions are involved. Perfect behavior in emotional situations is not the norm. That is why the *I Ching* stresses the virtue of fairness. You have to date the right person.

The yin trigram (the girl) is above the yang (the boy) trigram; the yang is making a slight concession to achieve balance in the bonding "game." However, there are three yin and three yang lines, stressing the equal role of both parties in the game.

Chapter 4

Laws on Achieving Greatness

Greatness includes fame, leadership, and wealth. While one can lead to the others, they are fundamentally different pursuits. The *I Ching* has sets of laws for each pursuit.

Although the *I Ching* recognizes the importance of security, it repeatedly discourages excessive wealth. Only two hexagrams discuss getting and keeping fame: Great Possession (number fourteen) and Concord of People (number thirteen). There are many ways to be famous but only a few ways to benefit the public with goods, services, or inspiration. The *I Ching* purports two ways to achieve fame: possess unique personal talent (Great Possession) or possess personal charisma (Concord of People).

In discussing the fifteen selected hexagrams, all trigrams are listed in the ascending order of individual trigrams, i.e. the fundamental trigrams are at both ends while the alternate trigrams at the middle in the group of four.

Achieving Fame with Personal Talent

Great Possession大有14

The theme of Great Possession is achieving and sustaining fame with unique talent and handling the rewards.

Elements

The elements in the fundamental trigrams are metal and fire; as fire melts metal, the message is inter-ruling. Achieving solid fame is about building individual strength, striving for excellence, and conquering all competitors or obstacles—including our poor habits, vices, and shortcomings.

What moral standards do we employ? The major body-part symbols in the hexagram are the head and the eye; the mouth also appears. The head symbolizes the great intelligence and wisdom needed to make quick decisions, the eye symbolizes the courtesy to observe and to accommodate others, and the mouth symbolizes the communication skills necessary to win approval and recognition.

The requirement of great intelligence is stressed even more in the alternate trigrams. Three of the trigrams are metal, two for the head and one for the mouth, representing a quick mind for strategic planning and good communication skills for gaining support. A good mind must judge what is in demand and decide how to fulfill one's needs.

The times to pursue fame are late fall, winter, and, to a lesser degree, the hot summer after the harvest; in terms of the day/night cycle, evenings and lunchtime are best. These are non-producing times. The pursuit of fame should be a pastime endeavor, a side job that does not interfere with our daily breadwinning jobs. We need to be financially independent to pursue other great things.

The dominant element is metal. Metal is the key to achieving fame. It is decisive, quick, fair, and solid. Metal conquers like a sword, sharp and decisive, with lingering vibrations that command respect far and wide.

Line Structure

Achieving solid fame requires three conditions:

- Having a unique talent
- Being centered and properly protected
- Being visible

You must have a unique talent. As shown, only one yin line appears among the five yang lines. With unique talent (the yin forces of knowledge and wisdom), a person with little physical strength can attract others and lead a society. This idea is compatible with the principle of non-contending, the central theme of the *I Ching*. Being unique is the surest way to succeed. In modern times, a unique talent could be a great look (stunning beauty or a compelling, comical appearance) or a great voice. Great musicians and singers have strong metal flow in their systems. These are some of the observations in my unpublished research on the cosmic energy system by the five elements. Over the years, I have studies people by groups of professions to gain more insight on cosmic energy.

You must also be centered and properly protected. Being centered is an equilibrium state; you are steadfastly anchored. The yin line is protected by two yang lines on both sides. How do you stayed centered and get protection? The principle of non-contending remains crucial. You need to do something that is very easy for you but difficult for everyone else so your market is protected from copycats. You need a unique product or service that is in great demand so others flock to you for help or service.

Finally, you must be visible. The only yin line (representing the person who wants to achieve fame) is line five, the highest secure position overlooking the other lines below. To achieve fame, you have to make your talent known to the public. Make a speech, publish a book, or launch a promotion to create visibility.

Commentaries

The symbols just tell us about the principles required to achieve fame and high position. The commentaries of each line supplement the procedures.

1. *Don't brag about your talent when you are in a low position. Be patient, and take the challenge to be quiet as a great opportunity to grow.*

   Line one is a yang line in an odd-numbered position (i.e., the right position). Thus, the person has the courage, the strength, and the right talent to start on his pursuit.

   However, line one is at the lowest position, and there is no yin line at line four to provide bonding help. The person has no hope for a quick start and should not waste his effort to show off his talent. Be patient, and wait for the right time.

2. *When you are entrusted with a job from a higher up, stay sheltered in a big rolling wagon to start planning to move forward.*

   The person has moved up to line two and got himself protected by a mentor; this is an excellent position. With a yin line at line five to promote his work, the time is good to market his skill.

However, it is not the right time to shine, as he is a yang line in a yin position. He does not have the right position yet. He may ride with the team, but he should stay sheltered and avoid raising issues.

3. *When offered a high position, accept it with grace and modesty. Never boast. Treat your colleagues with great respect and learn from them.*

With the right help, the person moved up one notch. At the top of the lower trigram, he is about to venture into a new territory (to the outer trigram on the top). As he looks around for guidance, he sees no bonding help from his partner on line six (a yang line).

He should take a temporary break to learn from other knowledgeable people in preparation for the next right move. This is a characteristic of a great man.

4. *As you move up closer to the powerful boss, you reach a danger zone of direct observation. Take great caution and great self-control not to stir up any suspicion or envy from the boss.*

The person has slowly moved to the edge of the new zone and is closer to the king in line five. Now, he is putting himself in a dangerous position for three reasons:

First, the king, a less powerful yin line, feels threatened by this advancing, young, capable yang force. Second, he is conducting business in the wrong position (as a yang line in an even-numbered, yin position), and he is vulnerable to errors. Finally, he is at the slippery edge of a new territory and unprotected if he does commit an error.

What should he do? He should keep a low profile during this transition.

5. *As you become a top boss, do two things: (1) bond to your subordinates with mutual trust and respect and (2) remain centered, or neutral, with your competing peers.*

With hard work, the young, advancing individual finally reaches the glamorous king position; the person is well protected between two yang lines and in an excellent position to lead the world. However, surrounded by powerful and vicious neighbors, he is in danger of being gobbled up any time if he does not play the right card. He must ward off jealousy.

As a yin line, he can never win with physical force. He has too much to lose to the surrounding barbarians. On the other hand, if he tries to seek help from one of these bullish neighbors, he will forever lose his independence. Thus, he can only win with a yin force such as intelligence or diplomacy. The best he can do is to stay centered to keep the bullies in check.

That was exactly what Switzerland did when it sought help from the United Nations (a yin force of diplomacy) to declare itself a centrally independent nation. With the right strategy, the yang (the big, powerful countries and people outside of Switzerland) flock to the only yin for protection of their assets. Wise people practice natural laws and win big.

6. *At the peak of your achievement, tone down your visibility by focusing on yin forces such as honesty and modesty.*

He has established himself as the top person in his field, and he could topple any time because he is the focus of jealousy. The outcome of this line varies with individual attitude and strategy. As a yang line in a yin position, he can maintain his status only by practicing yin virtues such as humanity, honesty, and integrity.

Variables

A quick and sharp mind, wisdom, great integrity, unique and great talent, good communication skill and observing power, visibility, bonding help

Laws

- Develop or possess a unique talent.
- Have the ability to conquer obstacles.
- Keep a low profile until it is the right time to shine.
- Have a clear sense of right and wrong to make quick and correct decisions.
- Seek the right help and move at the right time; while moving upward, practice grace and modesty.
- Build trust and maintain a neutral position.

Achieving Fame from Personal Charisma

Concord of People 同人13

The theme of Concord of People is attracting followers and leading by one's personality and personal skill, known as one's charisma. A born leader inspires great talent without possessing other special knowledge. He needs to attract people of various talents and properly position them.

What is his strategy for success? He should keep a low-profile to show his respect for great talents. This hexagram is the reverse of Great Possession, as the key line (representing the famous, great leader) is at the center of the lower trigram.

Elements

The fundamental trigrams are fire and metal, inter-ruling. The idea of conquering conflicts and obstacles remains true. Leading requires good control of other people. The body-part symbols show the head repeating twice, followed by the hip and eyes. He stays intensely calm (sitting) to observe, watch, and coordinate talents for the right job. He must apply justice, fair play (represented by the two metal trigrams), and good judgment. He must use the right people and reward them with benevolence and courtesy.

The animals in the trigrams are the horse and the bird. The leader can run fast and long and can also fly; he is flexible and capable.

When Concord of People is compared to Great Possession, one difference stands out: the person who leads with talent does not need benevolence. As people flock to him for his knowledge, he has the upper hand over his resources.

Line Structure

The line structure is one yin line leading five yang lines; no lines challenge the unique, great leader. Line five provides bonding help.

The charismatic leader should attract the best people with the top minds, people on line five who bond to his needs. He is honest and fair (symbolized by the yang lines) when selecting talent. No yin forces such as bribery are involved in any lines.

Unlike in the Great Possession, this leader stays in the lower trigram, humbling himself to attract the top minds for assistance like an ocean lying low and receiving water from streams flowing down the high mountains.

Commentaries

1. *At the first step, adopt an open-door and equal-opportunity policy to all who meet the requirements for the job or membership.*

    Line one, a yang line at the bottom, indicates integrity and honesty at the entry level. Offer fair, equal opportunity to all when hiring or gathering people to do the job.

2. *Avoid special favor to certain affiliated groups. It is not particularly harmful, but it hurts the bonding mechanism of group members in the organization as a whole.*

Line two is a yin line at the right position, centered and protected. The four yang lines above want to join his team, creating confusion.

Line five enjoys the advantage of being a natural partner. Line three has the geographical advantage of being close to the boss. Line four, stuck in the middle, might make a surprising move to gain some favor at any time.

What should the leader do? He should stay centered, ignore the bonding relationship (showing fairness), and focus on the right talent.

3. *Practice strict fair play to prevent competition among members.*

This yang line three, being so close to the leader at line two, wants to use his advantage of location to get the job but is apprehensive of the attack from the more powerful line five. Instead of direct confrontation, he sets up an ambush and looks for the right time to launch an attack.

What should the leader do? He should stay alert and remain firm and fair to fend off the attacks. Pay attention to competition among members.

4. *Your fair policy will prevent attacks from greedy members.*

Line four, a yang line in a yin position, inspired by the aggression of line three, is plotting to cross the blockade to reach line two.

The boss at line two should adopt a fair policy to thwart off the intention of line four and eliminate the need for the attack. There is nothing to worry about.

5. *When physical force is needed to stop the aggression, send your top talent for the job. Justice always wins!*

The top talent, at line five, is assigned the job to suppress the aggression for three reasons: (1) he is a yang force, (2) he is at the right position, and (3) he has a natural yin partner.

However, he is hampered by the long distance preventing him from reaching the hiring boss. What is the solution? The charismatic leader should give the top talent full support and promise cooperation. They should win with a joint effort. The *I Ching* insists that justice will win eventually.

6 *Don't expect to include all great talents in your team. There are always people who fail to connect to the group.*

A remote yang line is not connected to the organization and drops out from the social mainstream; he is about to give up searching for an outlet for his great talent. Regardless of our efforts to locate talent, we always miss out on someone great. Talented individuals must reach out for good opportunities. Have no regrets if you happen to miss out on some great talents. It is a natural course.

Variables

Courtesy, integrity, fair play, and the ability to accommodate and coordinate talents

Laws

- Play fair when designing a hiring policy that includes all good talents.
- Use wisdom and make a strenuous effort to reach top talents.
- Stay aware of fights among people near you. Never let them block you from getting help from the top talents. Your worst enemies could be those closest to you.
- Be aware that some top talents will fall into the cracks; as long as you try your best to recruit them, you should have no regrets. Individuals have to take care of their own destinies and reach out for opportunities.

Cosmic Truth

From the above two hexagrams, unique talent, inner strength, and self-reliance stand out as the keys to achieving high position and fame. Among them, unique talent is most important. We can understand how Lao-tzu got the idea of a non-contending philosophy.

While talent is largely inborn, we can always try to develop our innate skills into unique, polished talents. Start with a great idea. The efforts we save by not competing with others are worth the hard work involved in coming up with a new idea to market or share.

In metaphysics, a powerful element dominates the energy systems of those who succeed with a unique talent. Such a person has a dominant self and is in control.

Defending a Country

Leading a Troop 帥 7

```
━━━━    ━━━━
━━━━    ━━━━
━━━━    ━━━━
━━━━    ━━━━
━━━━    ━━━━
━━━━━━━━━━━━
```

The Chinese name, 帥, of the hexagram means "top-ranking general." It refers to a chief leading the troops to protect the country. A "general" could be a national leader. In the past, an emperor might have to lead troops to the battlefield on critical occasions.

The enemy is coming from the front line, and all citizens in the homeland are of one mind and one heart, ready to defend their beloved country. The only yang line is the leader; he is powerful, sturdy, centered, and protected, and he has a non-contending advantage. Fighting a battle takes physical strength, so a yang line is used to symbolize the leader.

This leader stays in the lower trigram (representing the homeland) where he is safe. He avoids the king position at line five, as it is in the war zone.

Elements

The elements in the two fundamental trigrams are water and earth, inter-ruling. Protecting the country is a matter of conquering the enemy. There is a saying in China that "when an oncoming flood roars in, block it with earth." It is a rule about the interaction of the five elements.

While water can represent danger or resources, earth can respond in different ways. In these trigrams, water stays below the earth and is confined by it. In this case, the earth is protecting the national resource.

The body parts shown are the ear, foot, and abdomen, representing intelligence, kindness, and integrity. A leader needs wisdom to listen, to plan, and to take decisive action when necessary. The leader has the capacity to absorb and contain the opposite force. Hands, mouth, and hips are not used in the symbols.

Line Structure

There is one yang line leading five yin lines in the hexagram, meaning there is no contending force to challenge the position of the leader. The yang line (physical power) is centered and protected. A leader has to be fair, indifferent, justified in every act, and protected.

The yin lines represent strategy, mental force, and respectful or submissive subjects. With an imposing physical presence, the leader is using a subtle strategy to conquer the enemy.

There is only one bond between lines two and five. The leader shows great confidence; discretion protects the winning strategy. The leader only confers with his top aides at line five when necessary.

Commentaries

1. *Set rules for the soldiers and the people, making them clear and loud.*

    The first line signifies the initial step in military defense. It is a yin line in a yang position, the wrong position; people bend to the need of military force to protect the country. Everyone sacrifices self-interest and obeys the leader from the start.

2. *The general needs a track record of outstanding performances and must be strong and capable, wise and fair, and fully entrusted by the king.*

Line two is the only yang line (the battle chief) in a yin position but is protected and centered close to home. The goal of war is to protect the people and secure the safety of the chief general.

He will achieve top performance as long as he meets the following three requirements: (1) he is centered and absolutely loyal to the country, (2) he is protected and entrusted by the king, and (3) he is respected by his key subordinates (the yin lines submitting to the only yang).

3. *His low-ranking officers should not take chances to venture to a risky zone; they would put the country in danger.*

Line three is a yin line in a yang position at the edge, a wrong and risky position, indicating a lower-ranking general who is overly confident and reckless and who underestimates the strength of his opponents.

The chief general has to be very careful when supervising his subordinates to prevent such things from happening.

4. Establish *your troops a high ground to get a clear view of the moves of your enemies.*

Line four is a yin line at the right position, meaning he is in the right frame of mind. A subordinate in a higher rank, is using a sound strategy and picking a high ground (line four, the upper trigram) for defense in preparation for a battle. What will the outcome be? He could win; his strategy is safe on all counts. The chief should not worry.

This scenario stresses the importance of a sound strategy rather than direct confrontation with physical military force.

5. *Never initiate an unjustified battle, but always put your troops on strong defense. When launching a battle, give the chief commander full authority.*

Line five is a yin line at the yang position, but it is centered and protected. This captain can be trusted to launch a sound battle. He has the top mind (the highest centered position) and the highest capacity (the highest functional line) to fight a battle. He is loyal (bonded) to the chief and the country. He knows combining yin and yang forces will achieve good results.

6. *After winning a war, beware of disloyal subordinates who initiate a power struggle on self-interest to divide the nation; never award them with land endowments or other titles. Take precautions to protect the nation from falling into the fight.*

> A yin line in a yin position, not bonded to any other line, represents a selfish person with the highest strategic capacity. He is unattached, not loyal to the country or the chief. He is, therefore, not to be trusted. Upon winning the war, such people should not be awarded with titles or land.

Variables

Wisdom, firm rules, strenuous integrity, and absolute consistency in ruling

Laws

- The commander-in-chief has to be physically strong and healthy, mentally capable, and objective; he stays back to be soundly protected.
- His high-ranking officers should be mentally competent and loyal so that he can trust them to make big decisions.
- Lower-ranking officers have to be properly supervised to avoid bad mistakes.
- Selfish and disloyal high-ranking officers are not to be given titles or land.

Leading an Organization

The Chinese name, 比, of the hexagram means "siblings in a family." The character has two equal parts. Siblings are equal in privileges and obligations regardless of their birth order. They are bonded to love one another and to live and work together for mutual benefit. All are obligated to help each other in times of need.

Leading Peers 比 8

The hexagram can also refer to any people of the same social origin or to any group serving a common goal. In modern days, it is an organization of any function. Regardless of its nature, the idea of mutual bond and benefit applies.

The hexagram illustrates the laws and procedure for leading an organization. While a general at war stays back in the homeland, the leader of an organization stays on the front line. Why? This leader does not anticipate any life-threatening attacks. Instead, he has to represent the group and be visible to others.

Elements

The two fundamental trigrams are also earth and water, but in reverse order. The outer water trigram on the top represents water pouring down into a container (the earth), signifying people coming from all over to join the organization to achieve a common goal.

The overwhelmingly heavy earth in the trigrams signifies a large, sturdy container with an unlimited capacity. The earth also signifies the integrity necessary when interacting with the members of the organization or clan. Water, which represents wisdom, is necessary but secondary.

Leading a diverse group requires non-contending skills and authority. The four trigrams in the body parts are the abdomen (twice), foot, and ear—representing great integrity and open arms, a deep and open capacity, and great tolerance for containing new members in a melting pot. directing and delegating with ease and listens to different opinions. The leader is humble enough to take action with fairness and honesty.

Line Structure

There is one yang line leading the five yin lines. The ideas of non-contending talent and authority remain true. The leader is centered and protected. The leader stays on the front line for two reasons: (1) for accessibility and visibility while representing the group and (2) to bond the mobile personnel and latecomers who are less bonded to the group. In modern firms, these mobile personnel could be the regional managers working in the field. The job of the leader is to bond the members to fulfill a common goal.

Yin lines wrap the hexagram on both ends, indicating the consistent yin force needed to interact with all members. Integrity requires an open mind, open arms, and kindness toward everyone. There is only one corresponding pair, the leader and his top aides. Thus, all members follow one leader.

Commentaries

1. *Practice fairness to recruit members all the way, just as a jar contains the same wine all along. This is the fortunate move to achieve great results.*

   Line one is a yin at a yang position, joining the other three yin lines as a happy team. The yang is bending to the yin, trying to fit in with the other members.

2. *The chief assistant to the leader should treat all members with sincere care and integrity.*

Line two is a yin line at the right position, centered, protected, and bonded to line five, the only yang line, a natural assistant. To be trusted, the aide to the chief executive officer has to be fair, loyal, protected, and compatible. This is the first step in the process of leading an organization.

3. *Beware of dishonest members who are motivated to pursue self-interests, putting the organization in jeopardy.*

Line three is a yin line at the yang position, staying on edge and taking risks by approaching the leader for self-interests. These members have to be avoided.

4. *As an individual looking for a club to join or a leader to follow, always look up and team with a great leader.*

Line four is a yin line at a yin position, a person with a good nature and a good mind and doing the right thing. This person is trying with good intentions to approach the leader. It is a fortunate move.

5. *As a leader, one's recruiting/hiring policy should be open, honest, selective, and voluntary. People are attracted to the organization on a voluntary basis.*

Line five is a yang line in a yang position, centered and protected (being a fair, well-liked, and well-supported person). Such a leader should attract members from all walks of life. However, expanding aimlessly or being too aggressive by including everyone who wants to join the organization is not wise. The leader should be selective, taking in only those who truly appreciate the membership or the job.

6. *Try hard to bond the isolated or off-site members of the staff. It is hazardous and dangerous to have some members feeling neglected or let free to pursue self-interest against the company.*

A yin line in a high yin position represents members or employees working off-site. They are talented (occupying the top position) and loyal (bonding to the big boss below), but if they are neglected by the leader, they might under perform or defect. The leader should bond with these great talents.

Variables

Discretion, integrity, honesty, wisdom, and tolerance

Laws

- Implement a transparent policy on hiring and recruiting.
- The top aide should be capable, loyal, prudent, and compatible with the boss.
- Watch out for the motives of those close to you.
- Reach out to the off-site staff, connect yourself to their needs, and carefully oversee their performance.
- Always stay centered in selecting/hiring members of your staff.

Building Wealth

Prosperity (Tai) 泰 7

Wealth building is a top concern for many people. Many people think they know how to get rich, so I will take this opportunity to discuss the laws on wealth in the *I Ching*.

The best sources for learning how wealth is created or amassed in modern times are the stories of the billionaires listed in *Forbes*. The major factors contributing to the wealth of the super rich are inheritances, marriage, and investments (including property, security, business investments) that require vision, knowledge, and connections. Let us find out how the laws in the *I Ching* measure up to this reality.

The meaning of the Chinese character 泰 is a "good life from success after hard work." The hexagram indeed preaches the laws of wealth building. The *I Ching* understands the importance of money and has a few hexagrams such as #9Hsiao Chu and #55, Feng, touching the financial theme. *Tai* is the only one specifically formulated on wealth building.

Elements

The fundamental trigrams are metal and earth. The elements are complementary; the outer trigram (earth) supports the inner one (metal). Amassing wealth requires support and good connections from the outside. Building wealth is about getting money from other people. In contrast to fame building, it is always a two-way transaction.

The basic moral is fairness to gain support and trust (like the enduring capacity of the earth), and a quick mind is needed to make right decisions a (like the chopping action of a knife). Your products or services should justify your profit. You need to stand behind your products to protect your consumers as well.

The human symbols are the head and abdomen, representing wisdom and tolerance. They also represent father and mother, who shoulder the responsibility of the family. The animals are the horse and the ox, the hardest-working animals. Achieving success takes hard work and great skill, more so than achieving fame or other greatness.

The alternate trigrams are the *Tui* and the *Chen*, symbolizing the mouth and the leg. Good communication is required during negotiations, promoting products requires leg work also crucial. Metal emphasizes fairness and benevolence to ease conflicts in business transactions.

Line Structure

Yang and yin lines are in equal number. As yin lines are of lesser strength, they are raised to a higher ground to maintain equilibrium. To succeed in making money, we need to put the other party on level ground.

All lines are in bonding teams; you need to be connected to other parties or to your customers and keep them involved in all transactions. But the lines are not all properly positioned. In fact, the two key lines are in reverse position. This means you must "put yourself in other people's shoes." Wealth building is about procedure of making money from other people; it is not about order.

Yin lines stay on the outer trigram to indicate the need for an open mind and for flexibility when connecting with people. A yang line on the inner trigram symbolizes self-confidence and integrity.

Commentaries

1. *Dig up the roots of the same plant, and let them work as a team.*

    This is the first step to setting up a business. The *I Ching* understands that having your own business is the best way to build wealth; no one can get rich by working for someone else forever. People who gain wealth from inheritance or marriage are exceptions, of course.

    The *I Ching* recommends that people with the same roots or interests unite to start a business. Joint effort is the principle of bipolar forces at work. Success comes from the interaction of the yin and the yang. No single person is capable of doing everything well. Just look around—you will find that many great firms started with a team of people.

    Line one is a yang line in the right position with bonding help from above. He knows cooperation is required to plan a joint venture.

2. *Move to a foreign land to set up the business.*

    To be foreign is to be different and unique. Imports stand apart from and above the local products, possibly commanding higher prices and generating more profit. Something foreign is often a unique product or service without competition.

    A monopoly can be harmful to consumers and to society, but it provides a comfortable profit for the individual behind the endeavor. Competition can become cutthroat. To truly succeed, one should stay unique as long as possible.

    Line two is a yang line in a yin position, bonded to the yin line above. A brave individual bends to meet the needs of the community to make a profit.

3. *Get ready to move to a new territory or to expand. Create new products or services to meet new demand. Before then, reevaluate your original teammates, and move forward without those who fail to grow at the same rate/direction.*

    Great success and profits come with regular improvements. Wealth building is not about emotion, soul enrichment, commitment to harmful relationships, or charity. It is about profits and assets. No business can afford to be stagnant or to be dragged down by counterproductive partners or workers. You need to remove any obstacles standing in the way of your profit. Line three is a yang line in the right position, moving into a new territory and getting ready to take a risk. An ambitious person is ready to expand in a new market and is revaluating his business.

4. *Take a break from profit making, and invest in research and development as you move to a new territory. Your temporary setback in profit will pay off soon.*

You need a new perspective to keep up with the times. Take time to understand your business and cultivate a new market or product. Spend capital to invest in long-term growth. You will recoup your investment eventually.

Line four, at the beginning of a new trigram, has arrived in a new territory; it is a yin line in a yin position, ready to make a correct move. Line four is bonded to line one, meaning the current conditions are connected to past performance.

5   *As you succeed, establish a kingdom, and marry your children to different outposts.*

You should diversify with new acquisitions as you grow. You need to branch out to new markets once your current market is saturated with your expanding services.

The big tobacco companies are textbook cases. The companies stayed strong after the tobacco business plummeted because their assets include businesses not involved in tobacco. Establishing acquisitions is a common and popular practice for corporations in modern time.

On the other hand, a successful enterprise creates competition; you need to diversify to protect your livelihood. When you diversify and expand to remote territories, you need someone you can trust and rely on.

During the time of the *I Ching*, people could only trust their close relatives due to logistic blockage over space. Marrying children to people in different outposts was the best and the only way to ensure the reliable control of assets.

Line five is a yin line in a yang position, centered and protected, and bonded to line two for support; he understands how yin forces work and how to get help by bonding to others in a new territory (i.e., the lower trigram, representing the younger generation).

6. *Build a ditch surrounding your kingdom. Try to stay there as long as possible.*

If you failed to diversify, and you are losing the market share to your competitors, you have to fiercely safeguard your remaining trade secrets and market share.

In the time of the *I Ching*, a ditch surrounding a premise was the most effective protection. If you try to sue copycats and fight them in court, you will be revealing more of your secret and end up losing more.

Line six, the highest yin line, is in an isolated position; she is, however, in the right frame of mind and will make naturally correct choices.

Variables

Hard work, fair play, responsibility, integrity, good communication skills, ability to compromise, flexibility, and solid professional knowledge

Laws

- Gather talented individuals who complement your strengths and work together toward the same goal.
- Develop a unique product or service.
- Periodically reevaluate your partners, and move forward only with partners who share your goals.
- Take time to conduct research and development.
- Diversify after great growth.
- Sit tight to protect your remaining market share when diversification fails.

Chapter 5

Laws on Social Relationships

One of the lessons I have learned from my practice in metaphysics is that everyone is concerned about relationships. Our happiness and success depend on good relationships with parents, spouses, colleagues, friends, and relatives.

Are congenial relationships the privilege of a predestined few? Great interpersonal and communication skills are largely inborn. Successful relationships are about understanding and accommodating the needs of both parties to fulfill a mutual goal.

Rules for achieving good relationships are well researched and documented in sociology. Marriage counseling is a common practice in modern time. While some rules have maintained their relevance over the ages, many have become obsolete. Human rules do change to meet new needs.

Succeeding in relationships takes certain qualities and chemistry. One must be smart, gentle, pleasing, generous, thoughtful, and sensitive to the needs of others. In romantic relationships, youthfulness and good looks are important.

In metaphysics, people born with a popularity star show the above qualities. Most popular movie stars or singers were born with such a star. They are well liked and are more likely to enjoy fame.

Well-liked people are attracted to different people to various degrees. Chemistry between the individuals is essential to bonding and forming a personal relationship. This has become the natural law in relationships.

Social relationships in China at the time of the *I Ching* were much simpler than in modern times. Most people were self-employed as peasants or small merchants. The government was practically the only employer. Working relationships were straightforward. Although there were causal discussions about leadership and society among officials and their subjects, no hexagram in the *I Ching* specifically addresses the laws of working relationships.

Family was the main social unit during the time of the *I Ching*. The book has three hexagrams on families: Dating (咸, *Hsian*, 31), Coupling (恆, *Heng*, 32), and Family Management (家人, *Chia Jen*, 37).

Dating: Choosing the Right Mate

Hsian 咸 31

In the time of the *I Ching*, free dating between young men and women was practiced. Arranged marriage was a later invention of the great emperor in the Chow dynasty after the *I Ching* was written.

Hsian （咸） means "vibration without the heart involved." People feel attracted to each other without deep commitment in their hearts. That is the stage of dating. The fundamental requirement for healthy dating is mutual vibration, not the lifetime commitment of marriage.

What is the proper procedure for successful dating, eventually leading to marriage? Let us examine the trigrams.

Elements

The elements are earth and metal. The earth (the boy) supports the metal, and the metal (the girl) enlightens the earth by loosening it. Dating partners should be mutually supportive and complementary to build a bond. Both the boy and the girl are young, the third son and the third daughter in their respective families, so they are in the same social rank and compatible in age.

Both parties communicate as equals. Because the yang trigram possesses greater strength, the yin trigram is positioned above the yang in the hexagram to compensate for its disadvantage during the dating stage. The boy is advised to put the girl's interests ahead of his own.

Fairness (represented by metal) stands out as the most important virtue, taking up two of the alternate trigrams. Integrity is fundamental and supplemented with kindness. Partners should be honest with each other, and they should treat each other kindly.

The father and the elder daughter play secondary roles. The young people should occasionally seek advice or help from their elders—the boy from his father and the girl from her elder sister.

The times depicted are fall, late winter, and evening, all non-producing times. Dating game should be conducted in our spare time, not interfering with our working schedule.

While humans can date for many reasons and proceed in many ways, healthy dating with happy consequences follows the natural laws. Social gaps, selfishness, significant age differences, overindulgence, and misguided passion lead to bad relationships or undesirable consequences.

Line Structure

There are equal numbers of yin and yang lines in the hexagram, stressing the equality of the dating partners. All lines are in bonded pairs, emphasizing the need for cooperation between the two partners throughout the process.

Yin lines at both ends represent an open mind, flexibility, and gentleness. The yang lines in a tight group at the inner center indicate sincerity, integrity, and unbending dedication and loyalty.

Commentaries

1. *Vibration is felt on the big toe. Both parties should feel attracted to each other from the very beginning.*

The toe is the lowest and the forefront of a body. Why does the *I Ching* demand vibration on the toe? The gesture is symbolic, stressing the need for chemistry between the individuals from the beginning, taking place in the most unlikely spot. For successful dating, the *I Ching* preaches the importance of chemistry in developing a bond.

Line one is a yin line in an odd-numbered position, bonded to line four; it is a bad time to make a move, but there is good potential. Take a wait-and-see attitude.

2. *Vibration at the lower leg indicates good fortune; however, do not take any action/move.*

There is deepening emotion between the partners as vibrations advance forward and upward. Line two is a yin line in the right position. It is bonded to line five, the yang partner.

Why does the *I Ching* caution against any action? The vibration is not strong enough (represented by the lower leg) to warrant a good, bonded relationship. Coupling is a big challenge for humans.

3. *Vibration has advanced to the hip; do not take further action. Bad consequences will accompany the move/action.*

A yang line in the right position represents a deepening, mutual vibration; it should be an optimal time for the young man to propose to the bonding yin partner waiting on line six.

The *I Ching*, however, warns no. Why? The bonding process is only halfway through. More chemistry will create a more secure bond. The yin line (his bonding mate) is separated from him by two other yang lines in between. There are barriers to conquer! Take good notes before you leap.

4. *Vibration has reached the heart. However, the young man, for some reason, paces up and down, unable to make up his mind.*

Is it the right moment to propose? Line four is at the center of the three yang lines, symbolizing the heart, the most central, most sensitive part of the person. Therefore, the very powerful vibration calls for a decisive move toward marriage. What are the concerns?

The yang line is in a yin position, which causes the concern. The *I Ching* again signals a resounding no. Regardless of the intense emotion, anytime you are holding some concerns, wait for the dust to clear. Living together is lifetime commitment.

5. *Vibration has reached the back. When you feel vibration at the back, you know you have the right person as your partner, and it is the right time to take action.*

    The yang line is in a yang position, indicating the perfect time to propose to the yin line below (at line two). The back is one of the most insensitive areas and unable to feel vibration. If vibration reaches the back, it is spilling all over the body, a powerful, reassuring sign. Such powerful chemistry should signal a right move.

6. *Vibrations from the lips and tongue are not reactions of bonding chemistry. Clever languages alone are not good vibration. It is cheating. We should not take it as a sign for going into a permanent partnership.*

    Line six is a yin line in a yin position on the top of the mouth trigram and using a pleasing language to bond with both lines three and five. It does not create a bond, however, as that is against the principles of dating.

Variables

Good communication, individual chemical interaction and bonding, gentleness, integrity, and wisdom from elders

Laws

- Dating partners have bonding chemistry.
- Parties should be compatible in age, capacity, and social rank.
- Both should be mutually supportive, honest, and fair.
- The bonding chemistry should become an irresistible force.
- Seek guidance from your close elder relatives during the process from time to time.
- Chemistry is more important than sweet talk.

Cosmic Truth:

These laws are the metaphysics of love. They combine convenience and passion in dating. Exactly what is vibration? It has puzzled both scientists and philosophers.

From the metaphysical point of view, vibration is caused by the complementary cosmic flow interacting between the two individuals. The energy system (vitality, endowments) of every human is a product of the five elements; unfortunately, the composition of the five elements in any individual is practically never in equilibrium.

If we find someone carrying the missing portion of an element that would complement the harmony of our energy, we are naturally attracted to and eventually fall in love with this person. When two individuals find their missing elements in the other's system, they are attracted to one another. As they get closer to each other, the complementary interaction intensifies and grows into passion.

The outcome of the interaction of the missing flows varies with their nature and strength; it subsequently determines the intensity of the vibration between the individuals. The intensity of the interaction, of course, determines the power of the chemistry. More powerful chemistry produces stronger bonds. That is why the *I Ching* professes that powerful vibrations are essential to the dating process.

But why does passion evaporate, and why do some marriages dissolve? Individual cosmic energy cycles change over time and are affected by the energy cycle of the cosmos itself. New elements set in to replace some existing elements. As the energy system of the married couple changes periodically beyond their control, the complementary elements between them can disappear over time; this triggers the disintegration of the bond.

That is why passion evaporates. If a couple married for powerful passion without consideration of other needs for a healthy life, then the marriage dissolves when the chemistry bond disintegrates.

On the other hand, if the couple married for chemistry and convenience as well, then they remain bonded even after the passion evaporates. Having a similar value system, a compatible support group, and a commitment to support one another bonds them even after the chemistry disintegrates.

Unfortunately, the ideal, comprehensive wisdom of the *I Ching* might not be practical in real life for some people. While some people focus only on chemistry, many couples marry only for convenience. Philosophers have been debating what makes a good marriage: passion or convenience?

"He who marries for love must live in sorrow," says a Spanish proverb. That was the quotation Schopenhauer used to support his arguments on marriage. Accordingly, he claimed that marriages of convenience are often happier than marriages of love. (p.319, The Story of Philosophy) How we date or marry is, of course, a personal choice; our choice, however, carries a price. Thousands of years ago, before these arguments surfaced, the *I Ching* combined both passion and convenience as the basic ingredients for successful dating.

Coupling: Managing a Relationship

Heng 恆 32
Coupling

The Chinese character *Heng* (恆) means "constancy and permanency." The character is a combination of two characters that stand for the heart and cooperation. The hexagram purports that hearty cooperation is needed for a permanent relationship such as marriage.

However, the Chinese character for the heart is used to express both love and hate, depending on its graphic form. In its horizontal form, it is leaning to the loving side; its vertical form leans toward negative emotions such as hate. The vertical form is used in the *Heng* hexagram. In the context of the *I Ching*, marriage is, therefore, conditional love mixed with hate. Unfortunately, the quality of love between the couple shifts over time.

The *I Ching* believes in mutual commitment and integrity between marital partners. Managing the different aspects of a marriage takes different strategies. Being able to adapt to change is the key.

Elements

The two fundamental trigrams are both wood, a team of the same element all in one entity, bonding with one aim and serving one goal for proper function and convenience. Happy coupling partners live as one entity!

The oldest son and the oldest daughter, young adults compatible in age and social rank, are represented in the symbols. The yang stays in the outer and upper trigram, serving as the leader and protector of the family. As you can see, the gender of the trigrams reverses that of the dating hexagram, indicating the leading role of the yang in a family.

The yang trigram (the husband) is the foot and leg, while the yin is the hip; in movement, the foot leads the hip. Again, the male assumes the leading role in the family.

In terms of nature, the yang trigram is thunder, while the yin is the wind, which comes after thunder. Put simply, husband and wife move together in a natural rhythm; the husband stays more or less in the front, leading the movement. There will be natural harmony if the partners in the union fall into this pattern. Otherwise, more challenges will arise.

The moral to apply is kindness. As a rule, coupling partners care for and forgive each other. The concern for right and wrong is secondary. Fairness only plays a supplementary role. How should you treat your spouse? Be forgiving and caring. In fact, white lies are necessary on occasion to keep the family in harmony.

Courtesies such as exchanging little gifts or saying a few nice words might create some good feelings, but they are not included among the ingredients of coupling. There is no courtesy trigram.

At the time of the *I Ching*, the husband remained the central breadwinner and decision maker for most families. Social change has not altered this infrastructure much. People in general seem to be happier in families with the father as the chief breadwinner although we don't have current statistics to prove this claim.

Line Structure

The yang and yin lines are in equal numbers, representing the equality of husband and wife. All lines are in bonding teams, like the structure in the dating hexagram; both forces cooperate for mutual benefit all the way. You need to keep the interests of our spouse in mind in whatever you do.

All yang lines unite to anchor the center of the hexagram, symbolizing the solid bond between the couple. Yin lines at both ends indicate open-mindedness, compromise, and flexibility, three attributes needed to cope with members of the household. Both partners are ready to bend to the needs of the other. Both partners should be gentle to the other.

Commentaries

1. *At the beginning of the marriage, move with caution on bonding matters; blindly pursuing one's licensed right will result in bad consequences.*

    Line one is a yin line in a low, odd-numbered position. This calls for caution. A marriage license does not guarantee pursuit of our full rights as the husband or wife. Other unforeseeable issues could stand between you and your spouse as truly bonded partners. A newlywed needs a deeper understanding of the marriage environment and a deeper bond with his or her spouse before making sound decisions.

    Little knowledge and shallow bonds put us in disadvantageous positions. What obstacles stand in the way? Line one (a yin line, the wife) bonds with line four (the husband), and two more yang lines block the bride from bonding with her husband.

    The woman has to relate well to the other relatives to gain their approval and good will in order to clear her way to a beautiful union with her spouse. In the modern days, the obstacles could be the in-laws, the stepchildren, and the hidden habits of the spouse. She must make careful adjustments to earn their trust.

2. *Proceed with a moderate attitude and move with modesty; it will bring good fortune.*

    Line two is a yang line at the yin position but centered. This scenario is about the husband's role. He is centered (prudent enough to do the right thing) and protected (so he will not commit errors). The husband is empathizing with the other gender; he is trying hard to relate to his partner. He also moves properly and gets support from all parties.

    This yang line mates with the yin at line five, but two yang lines are more accessible to his bride. They symbolize potential new temptations and threaten the marriage.

3. *Losing consistency to stay centered would cause self-inflicted insult or shame.*

Line three is a yang line in the yang position at the edge of the trigram. The marital partner gets impatient and exposes himself to a dangerous circumstance. He is emboldened to change course. The *I Ching* says such a move would be immature and cause undesirable consequences.

4. *If you don't get results after all the hard work to make the partnership work, consider viable options.*

Line four is a yang line in a yin position, in a new territory, and separated from his natural bride at line one by two more yang lines. Bonding to the first line remains a difficult job. The individual, after much hard work and sacrifice, is not getting a supportive spouse. At this point, the individual should be convinced that the relationship might not work and should consider other options. Change is in the picture.

5. *A point of revelation: when your continuous, strenuous effort to bond to your partner is not giving you a good marriage, you need to make a decision about changing course. Here are the considerations:*

1) If you are a dependent and the provision from your spouse is your only source of livelihood, accept the conditions, adapt, and happily live with them. Get yourself protected, and stay flexible.

2) If you are the provider or are financially independent, consider the circumstance unfair or unfulfilling. To stay in such a relationship permanently would have bad consequences.

Line five is a yin line at the yang position but centered (a person capable of good reason but staying in an unfavorable situation) and having problems bonding with line two. There are three options: bond instead with the yang line in line four, move to a higher level to explore other options, or prepare to endure the hardship. It is all a matter of personal choice and responsibility.

6. *An unconditional, rigid commitment to an unrewarding relationship is a great misfortune.*

Line six is a yin line in a yin position, a right position. It is not protected and is vulnerable to drastic, negative changes. Her natural spouse is yang line three, which is closer to another yin line (another female, attraction, or threat to her well-being). She apprehends the possibility of losing or deserting her spouse. She needs to make a choice one way or the other. The scenario is complicated. Change is in order. As a yin line in a yin position, she knows to correctly choose to look after her own good. However, the decision is up to the individual. Any decision should be in tune with the truth that nothing is permanent.

Variables

Compatible rank and age, mutual interest and a common goal, mutual care, wisdom to switch course when needed, and trust

Laws

- Martial partners should be compatible in age and social rank; they should bond to achieve the same goal, moving together.
- Kindness, caring, and fairness are fundamental to the relationship.
- Try hard to do your share of making a marriage work, understand your partner (and his or her relatives), and accommodate his or her needs by all means.
- When encountering an unrewarding relationship, look for options; committing to a bad relationship forever is inviting misfortune.

Cosmic Truth

The metaphysics of marriage is change. Marriage changes with the cycle of the five elements in our systems. Passion between two individuals starts with the complementary bond between their energy systems.

As the cycle of the cosmic system changes every few years, passion between the couple weakens. Marriage is then about fulfilling mutual need and commitment. Passion could be reignited occasionally in some cases from new input of similar, favorable energy, depending on the cycle and the nature of the cosmic energy; the possibilities vary with individual energy systems.

The need for passion or renewed passion varies with individuals, depending on the stability of their energy systems. Strong mutual need (convenience) of marital partners would keep a stable marriage. The *I Ching* knows how the cosmic flow works and preaches kindness, hard work, and self-restraint as the keys to maintaining a good marriage.

Marriage is about fulfilling a common goal. It is a natural unity of the yin and yang forces, promoting growth, benefit, or well-being of both parties. Cooperation between the yin and the yang is the only way for everyone to grow.

The *I Ching* encourages the interaction of yin and yang forces. This is the key heart of metaphysics. Forgiveness and kindness (as the trigrams in the hexagram indicate) should dominate as the fundamental mechanisms for maintaining a good relationship.

Marital partners should accept the cosmic reality that clashing energy does occur during the partnership, as individual cosmic energy cycle changes. At times the cosmic energies between the couple could clash into each other and the effects could be deadly in some cases. This phenomenon might seem mysterious and incredible; it has been, however, an established fact among knowledgeable Chinese. In fact, that was the base, ancient Chinese use to arrange a marriage for their children.

How do we manage the difficult periods when the energy of one partner clashes with the other? Clashing energy could be harmful and even deadly. The couple needs a temporary separation, a cooling-off period, to avoid the clashing energy. As the cosmic cycle goes, the clashing flow may last from one to five years. There are formulas to calculate the occurrence of the clashing and its duration. The *I Ching* is about making proper changes and considering options.

In the *I Ching*, *Heng* is followed by Retreat, which is followed by Great Progress. The clashing couple retreats to recuperate. After the retreat, both partners can restore their energy and start over, making progress again.

The separation can be minimized not to affect the children in the family. It can consist of separate bedrooms for the partners, dining apart most of the time, or taking separate vacations. Reading a book alone for a few hours a day can also produce the separation effects. The goal is to minimize the interaction of the clashing energy between the partners so they can avoid a harmful outcome.

Metaphysical truth reveals that having a supportive spouse is the blessing of a privileged few. A great spouse is a gift from God, something attached to our birth system (i.e., in our "spouse palace," as metaphysicians put it). While a few people enjoy great marriages and the amazing blessing of a wonderful spouse, many are braving challenging relationships. While divorce is unavoidable for some, we should keep all options open.

Managing a Family

Chia Jen 家人 37

The character for this hexagram means "family members." The theme is family management. The four trigrams do not include the parents or the oldest son and the youngest daughter. Instead, they show only middle-ranking siblings.

Siblings compete with one another in a large family; those at the two ends, the oldest son or the youngest daughter, are normally not involved in the fight. Most problems stem, in fact, from the middle group, fighting with similar strength and competing for the limited resources and power

Managing a family is about keeping members in place.

Elements

The fundamental trigrams are wood and fire, interbreeding, with wood supporting the fire. Among the trigrams are water, fire, and wood, in a chain of inter-controlling and mutually supportive systems. Water can extinguish fire, and fire can burn up wood. On the other hand, water could support the wood, which in turn supports the fire.

Siblings keep one another in check regarding the family resources and compete for attention from their parents; on the other hand, they also support one another in times of need. The relationship is never smooth, and keeping the conflicts in order requires skill.

Moral virtues are courtesy (twice in the *Li* trigrams, meaning it is most important), wisdom, and kindness. Members in the family should look one another in the eyes when ironing out differences. It takes wisdom to function smoothly in a family; do not assume that all members will be loving and caring all the time. Wisdom and courtesy go a long way.

Line Structure

The number of yang lines doubles the yin lines. Rules and discipline (yang) are more important than tactics (yin) in sibling relationships. While husband and wife unite to achieve a common goal, children in a family pursue separate interests and goals according to their different talents. Protecting personal space becomes the most critical issue for family members.

Yang lines frank both ends of the hexagram; members should join hands to differences. Two yin lines stay inside at separate locations; members need personal space to keep their emotions intact and private. Every member of the family needs his or her own space in the family home.

Unlike the hexagrams on dating and coupling, this hexagram features only two bonding lines; they are at the early and middle stages of development of the family. Members work together while they are relatively young and pursue independent goals as they get older.

The two key lines (two and five), one yang and one yin, are properly located. The father (the yang) is on the outer trigram, protecting and issuing orders and reaching to the lower trigrams. The mother (the yin) is on the lower trigram, serving and carrying out orders and taking charge of domestic issues. Both are centered and protected; the parents are fair and fully respected by the children, and their authority to manage the family remains unchallenged.

Commentaries

1. *The first step in managing a family is building up a solid fence of firm rules to protect the family.*

    Yang line one is in the right position at the bottom of the hexagram. Being firm and establishing rules is the first correct step.

2. *The mother takes a central position on domestic issues to prepare proper food for the family.*

    Line two is a yin line in a yin position, centered and protected (doing the right thing and being respected) and using yin virtues to perform a female role. It is in the lower trigram, the domestic domain.

3. *Parents need to apply strict discipline to children when necessary. It is always safer to use strict discipline, even to the point of inducing temporary pain in the children, rather than spoil them with lax rules. The lax rules might give them momentary fun and happiness but will lead to bad consequences in their adult lives.*

    Line three is a yang line in the right position, powerful and risk prone. It is properly positioned between two yin lines. It is also the divider of the two trigrams, symbolizing the territory between childhood and adulthood.

4. *Have everyone in the household happily fulfill daily chores; it is vital to train children in survival skills and to enrich the family wealth as well.*

    A yin line in a yin position, bonded to three yang lines, indicates the power of unity. A person in the right mind leads the family members to work toward the same goal. Unity is power, the first valuable lesson for group survival.

5. *The head of the household (typically the father) should get in touch properly with all members to show his care from time to time, making sure that all members care for one another.*

    Line five is a yang line, strong and healthy, centered (fair and in the right mind), protected (respected and performing properly), and bonded to the lower-ranking members. He is fair, caring, and capable of providing for the family. That is the role of a father.

6. *Elders in the family should become role models for younger members.*

Line six is a yang line in the highest yin position. The highest-ranking member understands his leadership role; he is switching to another position for the benefit of the family.

The leadership model applies to all older members of the family, including older siblings.

Variables

Transparent rules, courtesy, sharing and caring, individual roles, fairness, elders as role models.

Laws

- Set up clear rules for family members and apply them consistently.
- Use strict discipline, if necessary, to ensure proper behavior among the children.
- The father leads and provides; the mother fulfills domestic needs.
- All members share equally in household chores.
- All older members serve as a role models, leading younger members.

The family system has been undergoing changes worldwide during the last few decades. While everybody wants a home, many shy away from raising a family. Many would enjoy the safety net and the joy that a family provides but would find they pay too high a price. The value of family has declined, and the family system takes many forms.

Do the laws of the *I Ching* apply to the current family forms? Parental roles are changing, and the number of children in a family has been decreasing, minimizing the phenomenon of sibling competition. The effects of role models are diminishing in society.

However, children from families with both parents performing traditional roles tend to have more stable and productive lives over time. Rules to guide personal growth, discipline to build character and responsibility, and sharing chores to form good work habits among children remain fundamental to the idea of family.

Chapter 6

Laws on Managing Adversity

The *I Ching* understands hardship and suffering more than anything else. More hexagrams address hardship and difficulties than any other themes. People who habitually divine with the *I Ching* hexagrams should have discovered far more bad news and warnings than good news. The *I Ching* tells us more often to wait than to move; there are more red lights than green lights.

Knowing the laws for managing adversity and for waiting out a red light contributes to success. When adversity puts you in a depressing or confusing state, your need for guidance is even more important.

Adversity comes in various forms; I have selected four hexagrams to display typical states of adversity.

Getting a Good Start

Sprouting
Chun 屯) 3

We all start somewhere to achieve a goal. Getting the first job or earning the first paycheck is a strenuous process. The hexagram called Sprouting illustrates the correct strategy.

With its simple form and short, interrupted snarling strokes, the Chinese character represents a difficult movement or stumbling steps. It translates to "a difficult beginning," like that of young buds struggling to peep out from the thick earth to the open ground.

Elements

In the fundamental trigrams wood and water engage in an inter-supporting process. Getting over the challenges at a difficult beginning requires support. Beginners are too feeble to conquer difficulty without proper guidance.

In the alternate trigrams, two earth trigrams anchor the roots of plants. In the beginning, we need to put aside our pride and accept guidance. The ingredients for the growth of the plant are there, but success demands a combination of good timing and favorable help. Among the trigrams is a single mother with three sons of different ranks, lacking leadership from a father. There were no girls in this male-dominated society; men were the breadwinners.

The oldest son (in the lower trigram, symbolizing the foot and leg) stands steadfastly on the ground, poised to move. However, while watching the turbulent water ahead (in the upper trigram), he hesitates to make the first step without the guidance of a father. The two younger boys want to follow a good leader. As they are active, young boys, they want to fulfill their ambitions.

What do they need to succeed? The moral in the trigrams reveals that leg work, experimentation (represented by the hand), advice and knowledge (wisdom from the water trigram representing the ear), and confidence are essential. One must have the determination to make a move, the intelligence to act at the right time and seek the right help, and the confidence to endure frustration (signified by the two earth trigrams of integrity and reliability).

What is the right time for a move? It is shortly before the onset of spring and close to dawn. There is light at the end of the tunnel, so to speak. Waiting is part of the process.

Line Structure

There are twice as many yin lines as yang lines. Yin forces such as patience, elaborate thinking and planning, and getting help are important to success in difficult times. A yang line provides a good foundation to venture out. Another yang line at the higher level guards the boys from stumbling into deep trouble.

There are two bonding line pairs; we need cooperation and helping hands during difficult times. However, help does not always come. We need to prepare to fight alone when necessary. Three yin lines between the two yang lines indicate that we should move with caution in a "stop and go" mode. That is, we must move with prudence.

Commentaries

1. *Make a move regardless of the unknowns ahead when you have the required training. Taking the first step forward is the key to success.*

   Line one is a yang line in the right position; the person is energetic and trained to succeed. Facing three yin lines above, he should move forward for the following reasons: (1) he has the ability, (2) lines three and four will provide some help, and (3) the road forward is open.

   That is, we take calculated risks (we "test the waters") when we are well prepared and when potential help is available, regardless of the unknown hassles. Determination to take the first step forward sets us on the path to success.

2. *Move toward the right goal regardless of the obstacles and temptations.*

   Line two is a yin line at the yin position, protected and centered. She is in the right environment. However, there is one drawback: the yang line (another male) below wants her to stay to be his wife. This temptation distracts her from moving forward.

   What should she do? She should resist the temptation of temporary comfort and endure the hardship of taking the longer route to unite with the right mate at line five. She should never look back.

   Do not get distracted by an inferior goal. Look forward to a bigger goal that is right for you!

3. *Get the help of a ranger when trying to hunt in a deep forest. That is, move with the help of a good guide when in doubt.*

   Line three is a yin line in a yang position, indicating that the reckless young person has ventured into a risky zone. She is apt to get lost. Why?

   There is no bonding line ahead. She is at the edge of an unknown territory and should gather information and prepare a roadmap before proceeding. Moving forward blindly results in misfortune.

4. *Move forward to a higher goal when opportunity knocks at the door.*

   Line four, a yin line, is in the right position and knows how to make the right choice. She faces a dilemma, having lost sight of the best direction. At line four, her natural marital partner is line one, a yang for a good match. However, she has moved forward in her personal achievements and become close to another suitor at line five, who happens to propose to her as well. What should she do?

The *I Ching* responds: It is good fortune to go forward! Forget the past! Turning back would mean starting all over again, a waste of resources. In career matters, the name of the game is advancement.

5. *Get yourself well protected before advancing into an odd situation.*

Line five is a yang line in a yang position, centered but not exactly protected in this case. Why?

It is surrounded by yin lines, representing deep water. He has moved into the narrow landing in the deep water all around him. His only bonding partner, yin line two, is of lesser strength and cannot provide assistance. Moreover, line two is closer to another yang line (line one) and could be easily distracted.

What should he do? He should stay put and remain calm. Reevaluate the environment, and seek the right timing. Retreat a few steps if possible, one at a time. The hexagram sends this message: look before you leap.

6. *A blind move is costly! Take precaution.*

Line six is a yin line at the top without bonding help. For some reason, the yang line (line five) fails to see the danger and keeps advancing into deeper water. He eventually puts himself in great sorrow and has to pay a great price.

Variables

Diligence, prudence, advancement, and self-confidence

Laws

- Make the first move forward to meet opportunity regardless of the obstacles and unknowns, as long as there is no immediate danger.
- Reach for the right goal for you.
- When in doubt, conduct research and make a plan.
- Aim for a higher, new goal if possible.

- Beware of the deep water. Look before you leap.
- Prepare to pay a high price for a blind move.

Cosmic Truth

When encountering difficulty, the *I Ching* laws stress preparedness, prudence, hard work, and, most importantly, getting help. Success is always the result of yin and yang complementing each other. When we complement our inner deficiencies with outside help, we create the beneficial interaction of yin and yang.

But getting help requires wisdom. The skill is a cosmic gift and only partly learned; it is a metaphysical product. People born with a mentor star in their cosmic energy are most likely to get the right help when they need it. And these folks rarely make errors in career matters and are usually prudent, hard working, flexible, open-minded, and generous.

Gaining takes risk, but risk does not always reward us with gain. Prudence in taking risk is the key to success. We cannot fight destiny, but we can pick up the proper attitude and the good working habits necessary to make our journeys more smooth and joyful.

Getting Daily Bread

Yee 頤 (The Jaws) 27
Getting Provisions

======================== ========   ========
========   ========   ========   ========
======================== ========   ========
======================== ========   ========
======================== ========   ========
========   ========   ========   ========
======================== ========   ========

On our treacherous life paths, we are sometimes unable to meet our daily needs. We are all prone to get sick or to have need of some support. At other times, we need guidance on how to best provide for the needy. *Yee* offers insight and a strategy for coping with such issues.

The jaw controls the movement of the mouth when we a person eats or talks. The theme of the hexagram is about controlling the intake of food, getting provisions for one's livelihood, and nurturing oneself with the right food during illness.

Elements

In the fundamental trigrams, the elements are wood and earth, and one controls the other. Getting well or obtaining provisions is not about mutual support; convincing another party to meet our needs takes skill, and we must practice self-control over temptations. Thus, it is an inter-ruling process.

Among the four trigrams, two yang trigrams stay outside at both ends, protecting the two yin lines at the middle. Two sons guard the front and back doors to protect the ailing mother inside. The young son (the *Ken* trigram), who symbolizes the dog and hands, is watching the front door, blocking intruders with both hands and barking like a dog. The older son, representing the horse and legs/foot, stays at the back door, ready to rush the mother to get help when needed without being seen by the neighbors.

Prudent people keep their weaknesses to themselves. No one outside the family should know about the weakness of the mother. The weak are vulnerable and need privacy and protection.

These are the *I Ching* laws for nurturing the sick: Take great precaution to protect the weakness (or sickness) from being known outside of the immediate family. The patient is vulnerable and needs to focus his or her energy on recuperating, not on receiving visitors. Announcing the bad news to outsiders would expose the patient to unwanted intrusions or attacks.

The thunder trigram stays low, piled on by a mountain trigram above. The movements of the patients are being stopped by the mountain. The feeble have to restrain from unnecessary movements and keep their motives to themselves when they seek help.

During recuperation,: caregivers must provide assurance to the patient that recovery is certain, and kindness (as indicated by the one wood trigram) must be shown toward the patient at all times. As implied by the three earth trigrams, the patient must be confident that he or she will recover.

Line Structure

Yin lines are double the number of yang lines. Blessing is yang, and sickness or any other misfortune is yin. Weakness, uncertainty, and fear are yin forces. In this case, yang is used only to protect the weakness, to cover up the fear, and to seal the motivation of the person seeking care. That is why more yin lines are seen.

Bonded lines are seen on the peripherals when outside help is needed. The two key lines are independent. Recovering from illness is fundamentally a solo pursuit. Yang lines flank both ends to symbolize protection.

Yin lines also represent the secret motivation, fear, anxiety, pain, and quiet emotions of someone in need. All have to be hidden or protected by a yang force.

Commentaries

1. *Restrain from tasty food or improper desire. Take the sacred tortoise as your role model.*

   Line one is a yang line at the right position, confident and aggressive, with four yin lines above competing to pair up with it. In this scenario, the yin lines symbolize good food and other vices. This person is being tempted on all fronts.
   The *I Ching* warns that he should take the sacred tortoise as a role model, which can survive without food for many days. If he refuses to restrain himself, he is bringing on great misfortune.

2. *Restrain from getting the wrong mate as a provider.*

   Line two presents a different theme: a woman needs a mate as a provider. This is a yin line in a yin position but without a bonding mate. Surrounded by other women (three more yin lines), she desperately wants a provider.
   That was common practice among women in ancient China. Unfortunately, the options in her case are embarrassing. No bonding mate waits for her. She has to cope with these odds.
   If she reaches to the potential suitor at yang line one, she would be marrying someone of inferior status who does not qualify as a provider. The other yang line at line six is far more accessible to other women and is too high to be her suitor.
   The *I Ching* commentary warns that the potential misfortune of getting the wrong mate could be worse than having no mate. What should this person do? It is the choice of the individual. Use prudence and get ready for the price you have to pay.

3. *Using the wrong tactics/being in the wrong environment to get a provider will not bring success.*

   Line three is a yin line in the wrong position, vulnerable to errors. The woman at line two is advancing, trying to reach the yang line at the top.

All along, she has used the wrong approach; after ten years, she has not succeeded.

A yin line in a yang position indicates a woman using the wrong approach to find a suitor. Consequently, she does not succeed.

4. *Marrying a man of lower rank is challenging; it takes wisdom and strength to cope with the consequences.*

A yin line is in a yin position, bonded to the male in line one. The bonding team appears in reverse order. A man of lower rank is proposing to a woman of higher rank. Should the woman accept the proposal?

As a bonding pair, their common ground gives the green light for marriage. However, after a woman marries a man of lower status, she might be despised by her husband; she might not be happy after all.

Unfortunately, it could be her only option. If she makes this choice, she has to carefully monitor the relationship and prepare for misfortune.

If you have to marry someone of lower rank or ability for survival, you need to prepare for challenges. The theme also applies to taking an inferior job not matching your ability and training or serving an inferior boss; you have to prepare for the slight and for other challenges from a threatened boss.

5. *Marrying someone for the sake of feeding a group or saving a country results in good fortune. It is a noble cause.*

Line five is a yin line at the king position, which is reserved for the male. The queen is not strong enough to support her subjects, and she needs help.

She sits next to a higher and more resourceful yang line. But there is no common ground between lines five and six; she is not attracted by or connected to this man in any sense. However, this man stands as a great provider. Should the woman marry him?

If this high-ranking woman has an obligation to provide for a group of dependents, then she would be marrying for a noble cause. The union will result in good fortune.

Marrying for the noble cause of convenience is morally sound and personally rewarding.

6. *Use great prudence to be a provider. Being in a wrong position providing for a needy group takes wisdom to meet the challenge.*

Line six is a yang line in a yin position—a provider in a wrong position. It is not proper because he is not the king. Helping the queen provide for the subjects is the duty of the king.

He is in an awkward and shaky position. The subjects of the queen might be suspicious of his motive, hampering his performance and standing. What should he do for self-protection?

As long as the provider is not intruding on the authority of the queen or hurting her subjects, the consequences are fortunate. Thus, the intentions and the approach of the individual are vital.

Variables

Integrity, loyalty, prudence, and restraint

Laws

- Keep your needs and desires under heavy cover, and show great restraint.
- Seek help from the higher up if you need to.
- Get ready for challenges if you seek help from below.
- Seek help by all means if you have to provide for a group or a nation. This is a noble cause.
- When you help others, do so with integrity and sincerity. This is for your self-protection.

Cosmic Truth

"The higher-up Divine always protect/reward those who perform noble deeds!" This has been a recurrent law in the *I Ching*. Is there truth to this law? The answer could be philosophical. But it is truly metaphysical, reflecting that the *I Ching* is the basis of metaphysics.

In a Chinese metaphysical system, those who were born with a guard star in their systems are always protected by an invisible hand in times of danger. It turns out that these folks are very kindhearted, ready to sacrifice their own interests to help others. They normally refrain from vice. A powerful guard is usually found in the systems of noble-minded leaders.

Being a Dependent

Li Radiance 離 30
Being a Dependent

—————————————
———————— ————————
—————————————
—————————————
———————— ————————
—————————————

———— ———— ———— ———— ———— ————
—— —— —— —— ———— ———— ———— —— ——
———— ———— ———— ———— ———— ————

   In the past, being a dependent could be the ultimate fate of a woman who couldn't find a husband. The social system would not allow a female to get a good education, a civil job, or an inheritance from the family. In the *Li* hexagram, both trigrams are young women.

   In modern times, the same fate could happen to anyone who has some tough luck. As life goes up and down, we all need help at certain point on our life paths. In extreme, unfortunate circumstances, we may become dependents.

   How can one be a successful and happy transient dependent? The *Li* hexagram offers insight.

   Why is the Radiance hexagram used to deliver the message? A dependent is like a shadow, fragile and shifting or waning with the direction of the light (which represents the provider). *Li* represents the sun, the best source of light. (The word "*li*" means "sun.")

   Two light trigrams are used to show the rotation of the sun, symbolizing the transitory nature of a dependent. Life under someone's wing is temporary; no one should be a long-term dependent. The transit through this stage of life should be kept short, like the rotation period of the sun, if possible.

Elements

Two fundamental trigrams are of the same element: the fire and the heat. Being a dependent should be a transitional state: there is nothing to conquer or to support. The dependent has no right to ask for more than what the provider offers. The person is in a passive position, playing an insignificant role.

All four trigrams are young females of different ages, adults who have not yet reached motherhood. They have just begun to seek a provider for a family.

Dependents should show courtesy (a moral that appears twice in two trigrams), kindness, and fairness. How does one show courtesy? The hexagram illustrates with body parts: Observe the rules (the hexagram uses the eyes more often than any other organ), and do as the Romans. Sit down (with the hips), and stay in position as not to disturb the provider. Please others with kind words (kindness from the mouth).

Dependents show up in the non-producing hours, lunch and dinner time, and are considerate enough not to disturb the working schedules of their providers. At best, they should help cook and clean up after the meal.

Line Structure

In both trigrams, yin lines stay within two yang lines representing the feeble individual under the wings of the protectors. Yang lines are double the number of yin lines. Dependents have to be in the minority of society. Dependents play by transparent rules and do not hurt their providers with underhanded tricks.

None of the lines are in bonded pairs. The passive position of dependents does not require a partner. They are not to team with others to organize any actions that would disturb the providers.

Commentaries

1. *Search hard for the right provider. It pays to take many repetitive trips to compare before making the final decision.*

    Line one is a yang line at the right position, symbolizing a dynamic, forward-looking young man in his right mind, rightfully taking steps to improve his life and trying to get help.

    However, he is in a low position without bonding help from above, and getting ahead is difficult. He is busily moving back and forth, searching for the right help.

2. *As a dependent, get yourself protected by taking a detached, neutral position; be fair, reliable, and trustworthy.*

    Line two is a yin line at the right position, centered and properly protected by two yang lines, without bonding help. The dependent is level-headed and ready to make a naturally correct choice. She eventually finds her provider and puts herself in a good position under the provider's wings; she is detached from all parties involved.

3. *Older folks should not bother to get under someone's wing to move ahead. At their twilight age, they should take it easy and make the best of what they have on their own and be happy.*

    The last line of the first sun, a representation of sunset, symbolizes an aging person. As we get older, we should make way for the young generation to compete for its share. Older people should do simple things to entertain themselves; getting more than necessary at the expense of others would invite misfortune.

4. *A dependent should never harm the provider in any manner; it would be a great misfortune. The ungrateful person will be fatally defeated.*

    Line four is a yang line at the yin position, right below a yin line, symbolizing aggressive male dependent using improper tricks to attack a higher-ranked person. He is demanding more provisions from his provider, who is unprepared for the attack. He counts on his greater physical strength in doing the wrong thing.
    The ungrateful person will be fatally defeated. The *I Ching* consistently warns against vice, sin, fraud, and all unethical conduct.

5. *When under potential invasion by strong neighbors, use a neutral position to protect your independence.*

    This is a new aspect of the same theme. It is about surviving by protecting one's independence in the presence of vicious neighbors.
    Line five is a yin line centered at the king position but flanked by three yang lines, representing three competing powers. It is in danger of being gobbled up by one or all powers. The theme is preserving independence under the shadow of invaders.

As a small country led by a feeble queen, what is her chance of survival? She should stay centered and neutral, remaining alert to any moves from each side (just as Switzerland, surrounded by four powerful countries, declared itself neutral). She prospers as a result.

6. *Punish the rebel chief, but spare the followers (dependents); they commit no crime as dependents.*

This phase of the theme is about the principles of treating dependents. Line six is a yang line in a yin, but powerful, position. He is in a position to subdue and punish any rebels. He, however, should spare all the dependents or followers of the rebel chief.

As a yang line at the highest position in a bright spot, glorious and visionary, he should use yin forces to plan his strategy from every perspective to properly protect the country.

Variables

Courtesy, compliance, brevity, detachment, and neutrality

Laws

- Carefully and diligently locate the proper provider.
- Be polite, helpful, and grateful, and conform to the rules of your provider.
- Make your dependence brief and painless.
- Limit your need for help to your productive age.
- Protect your independence by taking a neutral position when threatened by neighbors.
- Do not involve the dependents when punishing the chief for misbehavior.

Cosmic Truth

In metaphysical reality, those born with feeble cosmic energy usually enjoy entitlement to wealth or success with very little effort of their own. They are, as a rule, very gentle, pleasing, smart, observant, and accommodating. They have little control over their lives and are prone to have ups and downs.

Any time they try to rebel and change their personalities to behave at odds with the people in their surroundings, they will encounter great disaster. What triggers the switch is the changing cycle of cosmic energy. The metaphysical system is able to identify the feeble energy system and predict the change, enabling the dependent individual to take precautions. Those born with two dominant, conflicting energies controlling their lives (such as water and fire) tend to behave gingerly and are extremely cautious when making decisions. They are trying hard to maintain a balance among the powerful forces in their lives.

Making a Move in Haphazard Circumstances

Chien 蹇 39
Limping

Difficulties take many forms and come in various magnitudes. Encountering difficulty is part of life. Getting out of difficulties often involves risk-taking, which takes wisdom and courage. How and when we take risk and how we manage risk makes a world of difference.

The hexagram *Chien* offers some guidelines on our strategy and attitude in six different scenarios of risk taking.

The Chinese character 蹇 means "immobile legs." Advancement is impossible in the face of insurmountable difficulty or danger. As the fundamental trigrams indicate, deep water (great danger) on the upper trigram and a high mountain (an insurmountable object) on the lower trigram block any moves.

Elements

The two fundamental trigrams are water and earth, inter-ruling, identifying a strategy for meeting difficulty. One has to conquer difficulty to win. It is not about mutual bonds, compromise, or support.

Among the four trigrams, water (the ear in two of the trigrams) is dominant among some earth and sunlight. When approaching a difficulty, we have to listen hard for advice, open our eyes to observe, and experiment with our hands until we solve the problem. We need lots of intelligence and wisdom from others, and we need self-confidence and some courtesy to ask for help. We must stay humble and flexible when looking for proper solutions.

The social rank of the four trigrams shows the middle son twice, the youngest son, and the middle daughters, all young people trying to fulfill dreams while encountering difficulty. No father, mother, or elder brother or sister guides them. We should try hard to conquer difficulties when we are young.

Line Structure

Like most other hexagrams on adversity, its yin lines double the yang lines in number. Yin lines show fear, anxiety, the deep desire to seek help, and the mental capacity to launch a solution. Yang lines depict self-confidence and action. There are two pairs of bonded lines. Fighting difficulty is more than a personal battle; it takes good help from others.

In fact, the opening commentary of the hexagram recommends seeking help from great men. These great men could be mentors who show us the right direction to turn.

Yin lines are at both ends to show that we need open minds and receptive attitude when listen to our supporters. The only two yang lines are separated from each other; we need to be flexible to meet challenges.

Commentaries

1. *Do not take risk in a hopeless case. Play a waiting game.*

   Line one is a yin line at a yang position, the lowest line and the wrong position, with many odds against him. To make the situation worse, there is no bonding help above.

After a few fruitless attempts to advance, the person decides to return to his original position and wait. The *I Ching* comments that he has made a good decision.

The right timing is the key to success. That is the cycle of the five elements. We get natural help when our beneficial element comes around.

2. *When you are in a position to protect a country, an individual, or a compelling noble cause, you have to battle the dangers with your life, without concern or consideration of the outcome.*

It is a yin line at yin position, the right position, centered with bonding help. A loyal subordinate (yin line two) responds to the call for help from the king (a yang line) at line five to fulfill a duty. Whatever the outcome, the decision to take action will be fortunate.

I am amazed to see that the *I Ching* is so sure of the outcome of a noble act all the time.

3. *Do not forsake your dependents to take a risk when there are no sure prospects of reward ahead.*

Line three is a yang line at the right position with bonding help on line six from a yin line that stays afar has little strength. This capable person in his right mind, with anticipated support from afar, is trying to take a risk. Should he make the move?

He has two concerns: (1) two weak yin lines beneath depend on his care, and (2) the helping hand in the outer zone is in deep water itself, being uncertain.

The *I Ching* advises him to return to his home to take care of the needy and wait for the right help to come along. We need to weigh the urgency of the circumstances.

4. *When in danger, gather help from your comrades and proceed together.*

Line four is a yin line in a yin position but in deep water (line four is part of the water trigram). This person is put into a position to defend a family or a country, so he has to perform. However, he needs to minimize his risk.

He should turn back to his homeland and seek help from his comrades, joining hands with line three, a yang line. Always look for help, if possible, when you are at risk.

5. *As a great leader falling into deep water for the sake of your country and people, keep your confidence up and stay centered. Keep up the good fight. A great, noble deed will touch the heart of the Almighty and eventually get his help. It is, therefore, fortunate.*

Line five is a yang line in a yang position, centered and confident with bonding help from line two, but at the middle of deep water. A courageous, great leader goes into the deep water for a right, noble cause regardless of the risk.
He could count on proper support from his subordinates. The move should be good, regardless of the outcome. God is on his side!

6. *Never wander to the far end of the danger zone. Always keep in mind where the great leader stays, and team up with the leader for help and protection.*

Line six is a yin line in a yin position with bonding help at line three. It is at the extreme end of the deep water with nowhere to advance; it is too late to get help from the far-off homeland (at line three). He has to use wisdom and try to join with line five, the next powerful line close by.

Variables

Seek advice, have perseverance, and show courtesy

Laws

- Do not take risk when you do not have the resources or are not in a position to do so.
- Do not take risk when support from afar is uncertain and when you have dependents relying on your support and care.
- Enter the danger zone when it is your duty to do so, even if it would cost your life.
- Gather all the help you can, and fight together when necessary.
- As a leader performing for a noble cause in a danger zone, stay calm and try your best; help will come your way.

Cosmic Truth

"The divine reward those who perform noble deeds" is a resounding rule in the *I Ching*. This is one of the reasons the *I Ching* has become a divination tool: it is mysterious and superstitious!

How valid is the claim? Apparently, there is nothing to lose in committing to a noble deed. A person is blessed with success, or a person enjoys a great name as a martyr when missions fail. Either way he or she is bountifully rewarded by the divine.

However, in metaphysics, the guard star also holds up the truth of performing noble deeds. Martyrs who fulfill impossible missions are prone to have a guard star in their systems. Such a star entitles one for help from the divine.

Chapter 7

Laws on Personal Enrichment

Personal enrichment is a modern term. It has quickly caught on as a fashionable idea, especially among well-to-do intellectuals. The term has broad implications and includes many categories, meaning different things to different people. I define personal enrichment as the enhancement or fulfillment of one's personal life beyond daily needs.

The *I Ching* was written in a simple society whose members performed simple chores to make ends meet day in and day out. It preaches good, hard work and good virtues as fundamental to a good life and a healthy society; themes on personal enrichment never stood out as important ideas.

In this book of the laws of the universe, no hexagram title translates directly to "personal enrichment." There are, however, codes mixed among the hexagrams on doing something for joy or fulfillment beyond the chore of earning a living.

In my diligent search for such codes, I found three hexagrams offering insight on this theme.

Education

Meng 蒙 4

The Chinese character for this hexagram means "being blocked" (physical, mental, or psychological) or "not able to see clearly." It could also mean foggy, confused, childish, or ignorant.

The person in such a state needs to learn new perspectives to clear his mind and make sound decisions. How do we uncover such blockage? The best solution is education, which opens the mind and broadens our vision.

Education was a luxury reserved for the relatively well-to-do in the time of the *I Ching*, as most peasants could not afford it.

Elements

The fundamental trigrams are water and earth, inter-ruling elements. To take off the blockage, one needs to conquer difficulties, ignorance, and confusion. An individual's effort can overcome the obstacles.

The streams flow over the mountain (the earth) down into a pool, symbolizing drops of knowledge gathering into a stream, filtering down to benefit crops and plants (serving others).

In *I Ching* times, written language (in the form of pictures) was in use, but there were no ink, paper, or pens. Each character has many cumbersome strokes. Lines and dots depict a picture of the object it represents. Writing a character was like working on a painting, very time consuming.

Writing was done with a manual tool or rope to form the shape of a character. It was an awfully tedious and painstaking process.

Schooling was exorbitantly expensive for the peasants and the small traders. Because only males were allowed to lead the society, schooling (preparing males for government jobs) in ancient China was limited to boys.

It is, therefore, not surprising to see the four trigrams consist of three sons of different rank and a mother but no girls. The mother was preparing the boys for school.

Students walked a long distance to school and then listened to the teacher and busily worked with their hands to tie the ropes or carve characters on mud or wood. As the *Kun* trigram (the abdomen) indicates, they were trying to retain all the knowledge in the abdomen, the largest cavity of the body. That is why the body symbols consist of ears, a foot, hands, and the abdomen.

The inclusion of young boys of different ages by the trigrams implies that education is for people of all ages; one can be a student at any age, as long as one is willing to learn. The correct time to conduct education matters is late winter and early spring, very early in the morning, the non-producing hours when farming is not performed.

It was common practice for students to take off from school to help out in the field during busy farming seasons. Maintaining a livelihood was always the top priority in the I Ching time of scarce resources.

Line Structure

Yin lines double the yang ones. Schooling is mental work (yin forces are at work). Study involves plenty of interaction between teachers and students and among the students themselves. But students also need to work and think independently.

Accordingly, there are both bonding pairs and independent lines, which show the dual message.

The key line of the hexagram is line two, which is yang, at the lower trigram, and centered but not protected. It symbolizes the student in his right mind to better his life, yearning for all knowledge far and wide (it is bonded to all three yin lines) and ready to venture forward. Line five, at the highest position, represents the teacher guiding students with yin forces.

To achieve the best results in education, learning should be purely voluntary; the student should feel the need and have a passion to enrich his life. In short, it takes a high respect for knowledge to benefit from it.

The opening statement of the hexagram proclaims that education starts with the student begging the teacher for help. To show his homage for knowledge, the student should steadfastly grasp the instruction as quickly as possible; he should never make the teacher repeat the same thing more than twice. It would be a disgrace on the student and a great disrespect to the teacher if the teacher had to say the same thing three times or more.

This foresight of the *I Ching* remains true today. How many times can parents motivate their children to study hard without the voluntary efforts of the children? Great scholars have to start with a passion for knowledge from the beginning.

Although slow learners deserve attention and chances to make up for lost teaching, routinely repeating mistakes or demanding repetitive coaching on the same subject matters would become habit forming. Such poor learning habits, instead of helping the students, just drag them apart from the mainstream of the class. Students have to worship knowledge, putting strenuous effort to grasp it from the very first step.

Too much pressure from parents or teachers has proved wasteful and a poor investment. As parents, we have the obligation to expose our children to different fields of interest to develop their special talents. After that, it is up to the individual child to initiate his or her effort to excel. They have to respect knowledge and pursue it with a passion

Commentaries

1. *Set up proper rules for the classroom at the first day of teaching and make them known to the students loud and clear. However, these rules primarily serve to maintain classroom order and to train behavior. They are by no means applied to hurt any student.*

Line one is a yin line in a yang position, without bonding help. It is lowly and feeble in the wrong position; it needs help from proper rules to stay on the right course and build up strength. The teacher has to seriously consider the consequences of enforcing rules when necessary. By all means, try to avoid using them for punishment purposes. In short, the rules should be clearly set up for discipline training.

2. *The student should take initiative to learn from all sources, like a responsible, good son taking care of the mother and all young siblings.*

Line two is a yang line at the yin position, centered and bonded to line five and pairing with the two yin lines above. He is a good student (obligingly bending himself in the direction knowledge leads him), respecting his teacher above, and he is passionate about pursuing all other knowledge available to him.

In modern terms, good students should diligently do outside readings after class as often as possible to deepen their knowledge.

3. *Students should focus on their studies and resist all temptations to distract their efforts. They should focus to study one field at a time, conquering the difficulties and mastering the details before starting something different. Otherwise, they could incur misfortune.*

Line three is a yin line in a yang position, the wrong position (the student is not in the right mind). It is unprotected at the edge of the inner trigram and bonded to the top line. But it sits closer to another yang line (line two).

The *I Ching* uses the analogy of a young woman trying to approach two different suitors at the same time; she is likely to lose both. The pretty lady, acting on illusions, greed, and wishful thinking (not in the right position or protected with proper guidance or knowledge) is closer to the yang at line two but tries to approach the male suitors at line six. Such a woman is no good for any man, and having such a wife is a great misfortune.

What is the message? Students who cannot focus on their studies are going nowhere. We need to focus on one field at a time, mastering all the difficult issues of the subject before advancing to another subject. Students who keep avoiding the hard part of a subject and keep switching into different departments are wasting their lives.

4. *What we study should connect us to reality; our knowledge should be in demand and benefit society, putting us in the social mainstream.*

    We see a yin line on a yin position, not centered, not protected, and not bonded to any yang line. The diligent student is studying hard (doing what he is supposed to do, like a yin line in the right position), but he is not objective enough (not centered) and does not have the proper guidance to evaluate what he is studying (he is not protected or bonded).

    He is well learned but has no one with whom to share his knowledge. Worst of all, he encounters no opportunities to use his knowledge; he can't earn a living.

5. *Education is a continuing process; opportunities and prosperity come with advanced and continuing knowledge!*

    A yin line is at the king position, centered, protected by a yang line above, and bonded to another yang line below. The student has advanced so far in his field that he has mastered the knowledge. Yet, he remains objective and receptive to new ideas outside his field (a yin line at a yang opposition, combining the pros and cons of all knowledge).

    What is his reward? He has many opportunities. This is illustrated by the yang line on the top nearby wanting to offer him a joint venture and by the yang line far away in the lower trigram (his homeland) offering a commendable job. The result is prosperity!

6. *A scholar should be committed to protecting his field of knowledge from improper infiltrations of fallacy or any wrongdoing from abusive users.*

    A yang line on the top protects all three yin lines below and is bonded to the yin line at line three. Yin lines resemble knowledge; this yang line has mastered his field. He is trying to embrace all the knowledge in his field by all means and is trying to protect it with the fierce, solid defense of a yang line on the very top, the outer source.

    To ensure his proper effort, he should seek help from his colleagues (the yang line at line two).

Variables

Individual passion for knowledge, integrity, perseverance, application

Laws

- The teacher sets up firm rules to train students.
- Students respect the teacher/teaching and initiate their quests for knowledge with passion.
- Students focus on learning and gain proficiency in one subject at a time.
- Students should pick a field benefiting and connecting them to the mainstream of society.
- Students master the knowledge of their fields with thorough effort and make learning a continuing process.
- Scholars should commit to protecting their fields of knowledge from fallacy and abuse. The *I Ching* indeed advises: hit the invaders hard!

Cosmic Truth

In metaphysics, what distinguishes a good scholar is a scholar star in the person's cosmic energy system. The elements of such stars are confined to water, wood, and metal, as depicted by the *I Ching* laws. The most powerful scholar stars happen to be water and wood, as indicated in the *Meng* hexagram. In reality, succeeding in great scholarship does take a passion for knowledge.

People with a scholar star sitting too close love to study but achieve no significant scholarship and make no significant career progress. These people happen to be too close minded to connect their knowledge to reality and too rigid to forgo their viewpoints.

Fulfilling a Dream

Ta Kuo 大過 28

```
━━━━━   ━━━━━
━━━━━━━━━━━━━
━━━━━━━━━━━━━
━━━━━━━━━━━━━
━━━━━━━━━━━━━
━━━━━   ━━━━━


━━━━━   ━━━━━   ━━━━━   ━━  ━━
━━━━━   ━━━━━   ━━━━━   ━━━━━
━━  ━━   ━━━━━   ━━━━━   ━━━━━
```

Ta means "big," "heavy," "above," or "great." *Kuo* is "getting across," "doing in excess," or "going over the limit." The hexagram is about principles of going over one's limit to fulfill a dream or an ambition or to complete a mission.

The *I Ching* understands our desire or need to test our limits and potential to fulfill our dreams. Every now and then, unforeseeable circumstances confer a course upon us to complete a mission. But there is a danger of going overboard and causing harm, hardship, or other damage.

Going overboard takes courage and sacrifice. How do we avoid unrewarding sacrifice, and how do we fight the odds? *Ta Kou* offers principles and provisions.

Elements

The top trigram is *Tui*, a pond with water; the lower trigram is *Sun*, the wind; they are the fundamental natural forces needed to move a sailboat to a distant land and the driving forces needed to fulfill an ambition. Learning to be a good sailor is an individual effort but truly succeeding on the voyage takes timely wind and complementary water, which are gifts from the Almighty and beyond our control. Fulfilling a dream is, therefore, a joint effort of heaven, earth, and humans.

Three of the four trigrams are metal, while one is wood, a downright inter-ruling relationship; conquering obstacles requires an iron will. One needs help from a metal force to make quick and sharp decisions, like a knife on a chopping board. One should also bend and penetrate like the wind, remaining flexible and open like the water.

There are two heads for wisdom and strategic planning, there is a mouth to convince people to act and to communicate, and there is a hip to sit down to think and attend to all the details of the project.

As the two father trigrams illustrate, a mature, responsible adult male can shoulder the job. Trigrams of young girls at both ends warn us to stay open, to move around, and to be humble enough to ask for help when needed. We are also advised to hide our big ambitions behind an innocent face.

The animals represented by the trigrams indicate that one has to be as meek as a goat to follow the leader and as nimble as a bird to be able to fly.

Line Structure

It takes great courage and a strong will to fulfill a dream; the number of yang lines doubles the yin. The four yang lines are united at the center, revealing the unity and unbending inner strength to hold up a dream or to expedite an extraordinary action; yet, we need to be flexible and open to meet the demands of others (represented by the yin lines on both ends).

Commentaries

1. *Treat your big dream with passion and fear but with great respect; worship your dream like you worship the mighty God.*

   Line one is yin line in a yang position, bonded to line four. The person (feeble yin force) takes up a yang position beyond his capacity, but he looks with great expectations and vivid hope toward the bonding help from line four.

However, his help is blocked by two barriers (yang lines above); the help is visible but far away and barely accessible. The journey is long and difficult; the uncertainty causes anxiety, but he is determined to move forward.

2. *Gather all possible help regardless of any obvious differences or conflicts as long as it contributes to your fulfillment. Stay centered; don't count on voluntary help.*

Line two is a yang line in a wrong position without bonding help; he is centered enough to be in his right mind, and he is protected and close to a likeminded people (the yang lines). Thus, he has the talent and the opportunities to collect help from his close peers. The yang lines, however, do not automatically come to his aid. He needs to ask for help.

Don't be too shy to ask for help. You can't make it on your own effort. The wind and the water have to be just right to move your boat. While many would drop a coin to a beggar, few would have sympathy for a big dreamer.

3. *Keep a watchful eye on every detail of your project; anticipate any possible fallout from your plan. Stay vigilant.*

Line three is a yang line at the right position. It is capable and courageous, ready to take the risk to cross the boundary. Though he is unprotected on the edge, he understands the odds and takes great precautions. As his bonding help lies in line six across two formidable barriers, he stays patient and prudent.

Don't expect peace while you are at war.

4. *Don't look back! Stay away from all negative forces dragging you from moving forward.*

Line four is a yang line in the wrong position, bonded to line one. Exhausted after a long haul, he is tempted to get the illusive help from the inferior yin line one.

The move is wrong; he will be pushed backward by the error. He should look and move forward regardless of what is going to happen.

5. *Watch out for a disgraceful help, and take precautions. As you need help to succeed, take it when you have to but with discretion. Prepare for its repercussions. It is something you have to put up with.*

Line five, after all the hard work, has finally reached his goal and occupies the king position; he is highly visible, centered, and protected. However, he got there with special help and with a hint of disgrace. As a healthy, able young man at line four, he married an older rich lady above at line five for the needed influence. The match is wrong, but it was his only option at that point.

He fulfilled his dream, but he has put himself in a position that invites disgrace. He has to handle with discretion and be ready to pay a price for his big dream.

6. *Prepare to sacrifice your life when the cause calls for it.*

Line six is a yin line at the right position pushed to the point of no return by the opponents (the team of yang lines) below; she knows what she is doing (playing a noble role, typically that of a martyr) and pays the consequences.

She is in position to fight an opposing team, and she is ready to pay any price, even giving her own life, to fulfill the goal.

Variables

Passion, determination, perseverance, humility, and self-sacrifice

Laws

- Be passionate about your dream.
- Gather all the necessary help to proceed.
- Stay vigilant in every move **in** the process.
- Keep moving forward only; never look back.
- Prepare to deal with disgrace.
- Be prepared to sacrifice your own life when necessary.

Cosmic Truth

While all the above variables and the laws on fulfilling a dream are irrefutable, support all of them with metaphysical evidence would be an impossible job. Bluntly put, when it comes to laws in the *I Ching*, no arguments would be sufficient, as no one can compete with the Lord.

Let me touch on a few more points. Solid inner strength (or iron will) is most fundamental. But will alone does not bring success. An open mind and a flexible attitude should be crucial companions. In the metaphysical system, four energy pillars represent the endowments of a person; fighters who score big are apt to have two solid yang pillars jointly staying inside and two yin lines on both ends.

Short-lived, brave martyrs tend to have all four energy pillars as yang lines. They are rigidly courageous, and they die before fulfilling their dreams.

To truly succeed in fulfilling a big dream, you need the Lord on your side. Big dreams shake the universe, impacting the kingdom of God you need permission to proceed. In metaphysics, the stamp is a mentor star in a person's four pillars of cosmic energy. A strong mentor gives powerful guidance as you fulfill a dream.

In some cases, a grantor star would also help. A grantor is a protector and provider. Most Nobel Prize winners happen to have their mentors or grantors aligned in their career palaces at the eventful moment. The winner of the prize for literature in 2007 is a good example.

Can we change the cosmic energy? The best we can do is to attune to it. Should we hold a big dream without a birth mentor or grantor in our energy systems? No one should be deprived of the right to pursue a big dream. Without help from the Almighty, we might take long, winding routes as we wait for his okay.

The Pursuit of Joy

Happiness can mean different things to different people and different things to the same person at different times. However, a universal definition asserts that happiness is satisfaction with one's life. In fact, pollsters use this criterion to measure happiness in people worldwide.

Happiness is an emotional response of satisfaction or the joy we feel. *Tui* is the only hexagram on the subject.

Tui 兌 58

Joy

The Chinese character for this hexagram is a combination of a hip and an open mouth; it means "sitting down in peace, talking, eating, or laughing." The hexagram is about how to be happy and how to make others happy. The *I Ching* continues to assert that hard work is needed to build a good life.

Elements

Both fundamental trigrams are the same; there is no ruling or breeding relationship. The pursuit of joy is a neutral and independent undertaking, free of constraints.

Both trigrams are metal, mostly copper, the most precious material at the time of the *I Ching*. It could set a criminal free or commute a death sentence. Copper was wealth, the greatest of assets. Pursuing joy takes a substantial amount of wealth. A person should accumulate assets before pursuing joy.

These two trigrams represent two ponds. Keeping a pond was a luxury in an agricultural society, a status symbol beyond the reach of the common peasants. A pond was multifunctional: it could provide fish for the family, irrigation for the crops, or water crops for the family to sell for additional income. Maintaining a pond took special technology. The skill required education.

In terms of body parts, there are two mouths, representing the act of talking or communicating. The opening statement is about teaching and exchanging words from the mouth. In ancient times, teaching was mostly done orally. Students recited lessons after the teacher provided instruction on subject matters.

Two mouths also indicate the sharing of food. Symbols from the alternate trigrams include the eyes and hip. People sit down and look at each other while talking and eating or drinking; that is, they share and exchange. These trigrams also mean fire, wind, and water; they contribute to a pleasant environment that includes warm breezes over the pond—very relaxing indeed!

The animal is the goat, a symbol of art. The humans are two young girls, naïve and carefree. The times depicted are lunch and dinner and autumn, after harvest has been completed. The virtues are fairness, with some secondary courtesy and kindness.

In conclusion, the attributes for joy are above-average wealth, some education, good life-management skills, a taste for art, a carefree spirit, a fair mind not to disturb others in the process, and, above all, the willingness to share and to exchange ideas.

Line Structure

Yang lines double the yin. Feeling happy or sharing fun are mostly yang matters. There are absolutely no bonded pairs. The sharing goes between or among the parties in the process, but it is not reciprocal. The pursuit of joy is an independent act. We are our own smiths of joy. No one can make us happy if we don't want to be happy.

A yin line sits at the top of both trigrams; people are flexible, gentle, and open to one another but stay honest and fair inside their minds.

A Global View on Happiness

Since happiness is a globally popular topic and most everyone desires to be happy, I'd like to take this opportunity to compare the *I Ching* wisdom with some global views.

First, we have to agree that happiness or joy is a transitory state. While some pain could be permanent, no one would feel happy from the same cause or remain in the same state of joy forever. In fact, a person's desire for pleasure escalates and changes over time. Regardless of its fleeting nature, happiness remains the ultimate goal for most people. Many people endure great pains over long periods of time to earn a small amount of joy.

Let us start with some of the greatest philosophers who lived close to the time of the *I Ching*: the three great thinkers in ancient Greece.

Socrates and Plato did not elaborate on happiness as a topic alone; their teachings did address "Good mind (education) and good heart (good virtue or clean soul) as prerequisites for a happy life. Aristotle discussed "Happiness" in great length as a separate subject. He argued that the goal of life is the pursuit of happiness. What constitutes happiness? Virtue, a fair degree of worldly goods, a good mind (for achievement and self control), and friendship are the foundations of happiness (p. 76–79, The Story of Philosophy)

We can summarize their viewpoint as: intellectual capacity, achievement, good heart and community spirit. All such conditions are found in the hexagrams.

Rome was a great, influential empire. What did the Romans believe about happiness? A proverb states: "Everyone is a smith who forges his own happiness." It confirms the *I Ching*'s nonbonding lines throughout the hexagram. Joy is an individual pursuit.

In countries like Germany and France, happiness is success and richness of mind. It boils down to good material possessions and education. In the United States, happiness is the full use of one's power and talent (education and self-fulfillment). Again, all of the above attributes are included in *Tui* hexagram.

What about the historic global view? Human perception of values has changed over time. From the beginning of the Christian era through the seventeenth century, people believed that leading a God-fearing life brought happiness. The *Tui* hexagram has double metal trigrams, symbols of justice and fairness.

During the eighteenth century the prevalent idea was pleasure (in the broadest sense). In the nineteenth century, happiness came from a balanced life (duty balanced with play, spiritual balanced with material needs). In the twentieth century, we sought a mix of perfection and pleasure; the prevalent view was that happiness must be attained by the individual.

We don't find any contradiction between the themes in the *I Ching* and the prevalent views from other great minds and eras.

The Reality of Joy

Let us examine how the attributes in the *Tui* hexagram measure up to reality. The best approach is to locate the happiest people and find out what attributes they possess. According to a survey published in *Forbes* magazine on October 23, 1995, of eighteen countries nationalities, Icelanders are the happiest people. Why? The organization suggests the following factors:

- Coping in a harsh, natural environment demands the cultivation of talent, skill, and willpower. To adjust to the extreme seasonal changes, one could be an accountant, a fisherman, and a nightclub singer at different times. It comes down to challenges and opportunities. In the words of the *I Ching*, owning a pond and having the skill to keep it functioning properly are privileges.

- Collective community support (a genuine concern for the less fortunate) and a pure spirit of sharing are vital. It is not unusual for Icelanders to offer temporary shelter to the needy.

- Hard work means duty before play. Many citizens work long hours and hold different jobs to accommodate the changing climate.

- Open-mindedness is also essential. Icelanders love to read and travel. Each person is determined to have at least one overseas trip in his or her lifetime.

In the same survey, poor countries turned out to have the unhappiest people. In fact, Iceland has the highest literacy rate and one of the highest per-capita incomes in the world.

Reality has proven that it takes a good education, a good income, and a sharing spirit to be happy. Although some people are born happy and carefree, sustained joy is based on security, which has to be earned with hard work. Duty before play is fundamental to a happy life.

Happiness does not come directly in response to our desires. As the ancient Chinese philosopher Chuang-tzu put it, "Happiness is the absence of striving for happiness." (p.96, The Pursuit of Happiness). That is, happiness is the result of man's effort on something else, such as achievement or doing some good deeds.

Happiness has never been a popular topic among philosophers or spiritual leaders. The New Testament of the Bible (the founding document of Western civilization) mentioned happiness just six times and never in a happy context, according to an article in the "The Pursuit of Happiness". As Hegel said, "The history of the world is not the theater of happiness. Periods of happiness are blank pages in it. For they are periods of harmony, and this dull content is unworthy of a man." (P. 279, The Story of Philosophy)

Hegel's comment supports the idea that happiness comes from achievements, as the *Tui* hexagram implies. The same idea is shared by Donald Trump who contributed an article on the Forbes: "The Pursuit of Happiness."

Commentaries

While the symbols and line structure discuss the pursuit of happiness, the line commentaries deliver messages on how to create good will and make people happy. The messages are part of the theme on joy.

1. *Being lowly and humble should not be reasons to stop people from making others happy; it would be a fortunate move as long as their motives are honest.*

   Line one is a yang line at the lowest level; it is at the right position but without support. The situation can be explained in two ways: First, a humble person sets out with an honest intention to please people. Second, a person of lower rank is assigned a job to perform good will. Both would achieve fortunate results. They don't need help to do a good job.

2. *Anyone with a good intention would create fortunate results in performing good will regardless of his or her position.*

   Line two is a yang line in a yin position assigned to perform good will; it is centered and protected. A low-ranking person is not assigned to perform good will, but he has the sincerity and good intention to perform, and he knows how to make people happy. The result is also fortunate.

3. *A low-ranking person, not in a position to perform good will that uses bribery to buy favoritism would bring misfortune.*

   Line three is a yin line in a yang position (representing a person using dishonest tricks); it is not centered and is unprotected. Someone in a low rank with limited resources tries to gain favoritism with bribery without approval from the boss. The outcome is bad fortune. What is the reason? One needs great resources (a high position with power and money), strong backup (protected bonding help), and a good reason (one must be centered) to succeed in bribery.

4. *When a high-ranking person is approached by a crook asking for unjustified good will, he should immediately report it to his superior and ask for protection from harassment.*

   A yang line is in a yin position, not centered and unprotected—an honest person facing poor odds in making decisions. He is approached by the yin line below at line three with a bribe. He should report it to the superior at line five.

5. *When the highest-ranking officer is approached by a very powerful and resourceful crook from above his jurisdiction, he has to stay alert and keep a distance from the crook.*

   A yang line is in the right position, centered and protected. This person, being in the highest position without the protection of a superior, is responsible for his decisions. With a yin line on line six above his shoulder approaching him with bribe, he is facing the challenge of confronting a powerful, resourceful person. He is in danger of losing his job.

   What is the correct strategy? As the highest decision maker, he is at the top and gets no help from anyone. He has to stay alert and must try to detach from this crook.

6. *When a powerful and resourceful person uses dishonesty to buy good will, the outcome is hard to predict. He could succeed or fail. Whatever the outcome, it is not an honest act. He is paying for the disgrace.*

   This is a yin line in a yin position, powerful, influential, and skillful enough to bribe someone for unjustified favoritism. With his great resources, he might easily fulfill his goal. Yet, the outcome depends on his target and on the circumstances, over which he has little control.

The *I Ching* says that the outcome is unpredictable.

Laws

- Be honest and sincere when building good will (making people happy).
- Dishonesty might work in special circumstances for the mighty crook, but it never works for the lowly, unprotected guy, as it takes great influence and resources.
- Stay away from bribery.

Cosmic Truth

What truly makes people happy are high achievement, a wealth of possessions, and hope—all of which increase the potential to make change. It takes a healthy attitude and capacity (a good mind) to have hope.

In metaphysical reality, a happiness star in a person's energy system normally makes a happy person. Curiously, the element of this star is always in the opposite nature of the individual's need. That is, when excessive fire energy is hurting the person, his or her happiness star is moist earth to absorb the heat; when excessive water energy is hurting the person, his or her star is dry earth to block the water.

Yin and yang forces balance each other. People with a happiness star adopt a realistic attitude toward the problems of life and are open to options, bending to the reality and adopting the realistic approach to solve a problem. They, therefore, eventually conquer the obstacles and stay happy. Chuang-Tze had a great point, understanding metaphysics!

Chapter 8

Conclusions

Summary of the *I Ching* Laws: Making Changes

In the "Book of Change," the laws are fundamentally about how to meet challenges or make changes successfully. The essence of these laws is summarized below:

- **Flow with the natural cycle.** Change follows a natural cycle, like the cycle of the seasons or the rotation of day and night. This rule of "yin and yang taking turns" applies to blessings and disasters, sadness and joy, war and peace, etc. There is a silver lining behind a dark cloud and sunshine after a storm, all in a natural cycle. Messages about change are indicated in every hexagram, mostly in the sixth lines.

- **Watch every turn in the natural course.** Downfall follows the zenith of great success, passion evaporates in a bonded relationship, and grace surfaces after a long struggle. Take note of how dynasties rise and fall. Be aware of your position along your natural course, and take precautions before a natural turn.

- **Do not become complacent.** Complacency invites trouble. Initiate proper changes to bad habits. Take a decisive, big step out of a hopeless situation to avoid being a victim. Take action at the first sign of change before a situation gets too complicated to manage. Remember the yin and yang interactions.

Attitudes for Change

The following five attitudes are crucial when making proper changes:

1. Engage in fair play.

Fair play is at the core of the wisdom in the *I Ching*. The *I Ching* acknowledges cosmic inequality. We are born unequal. Things are created unequal. Yin and yang forces interact with unequal strength. This fundamental inequality demands fair play.

For positive results, the forces of yin and yang have to coexist and compete on equal ground. The overwhelmingly stronger party has to make a concession to avoid foul play from the little guy, who is unable to compete with equal power.

The dictator has to provide an acceptable standard of living for his subjects to avoid a revolution. In a healthy society, people support the government. While foul play is dangerous and short-lived, the weaker party has to team up strength by collecting help in the fight for long-term victory. People eventually pay for their foul play. Getting help is a resounding theme in the *I Ching*.

2. Practice integrity with discretion.

The *I Ching* understands how integrity works and honors integrity with reservation. First, we should show integrity only to good, honest people. To keep a clean life, stay away from crooks by all means.

Second, we should show integrity only toward those who appreciate it. A rooster makes itself a nuisance by rigidly waking everyone at the same time every day. The rooster should change its practice to meet the various needs of different people at different times.

Even solid integrity requires change and adjustment to make it work.

3. Follow great leaders.

As defined in the *I Ching*, a great leader is capable, fair, and caring. We need good energy to make proper changes. A convenient way to get good energy is to borrow from others to complement our shortcomings. Learn from the wise, and follow the successful.

4. Use prudence to stay centered and to get protected.

Take a central position and buy time to get the right help when you cannot compete on level ground. Minimize loss by all means. Always protect your resources.

5. Know the limit for possible changes.

No one has absolute control of when and how to make changes. The Almighty always has the final voice. The rule of the absolute is not for us to bend. Learn to see what we cannot change.

The God-fearing concept is frequently repeated in many of the hexagrams.

Acting on Change

When making changes, follow two rules:

> **1. Avoid confrontation.** Confrontation involves two clashing yang or yin forces clashing; the result is mutual destruction. The *I Ching*'s laws are about yin and yang forces complementing each other.

> **2. Get the right help, act at the right time, and stay in the right place.** However, the *I Ching* does not give a clear answer about how to make the right change. The knowledge belongs to the field of metaphysics; it is a matter of cosmic energy, a hidden part of the *I Ching* and its laws.

Two exceptional metaphysicians unlocked the secret codes more than two thousands years after the *I Ching* was written. The codes and the systems were discussed at the beginning of this book. One of systems was introduced in my book *The Path to Good Fortune*.

The *I Ching* is highly intellectual and serious, demanding great effort and patience to understand. Knowledge of natural laws gives us an advantage in our battles, and most of us can benefit by adopting the right attitude when practicing the laws.

The *I Ching* as a Source of Inspiration

Given the nature of the laws in the *I Ching*, can we prove that they are the operating laws of the cosmos? Do God's laws provide a guide to a successful life?

An objective, academic evaluation of each hexagram would require a group of individuals with training in various fields. This enormous job, if ever possible or justified, might take immense resources over a very long period of time. How could it be done properly?

Only a perceptual and caring individual can appreciate the *I Ching* and connect his or her life to its wisdom. An official evaluation might establish the value of its laws and attract more readers, but it would make very little impact on my personal beliefs. There is no room in a laboratory for cosmic truth; for the majority of people, understanding the laws requires personal belief.

Over the last twenty years, puzzled by the mystery of life and fascinated with the laws in the *I Ching*, I ventured into Chinese metaphysics. I was unable to appreciate the *I Ching* until I had experimented with the impact of the cosmic energy of the five elements over many thousands of people across the globe.

The *I Ching*'s rules are the rules of cosmic energy. As I confirmed the truth on cosmic energy during my experiments, I began to marvel at the same truth in the *I Ching*; in fact, I am overjoyed and grateful that the *I Ching* had put these scattered rules in such a simple, marvelous, natural order.

I can hold this precious gift (the complete codes of the universe) in my hand and look, compare, admire, and be inspired at any time. Amazingly, these laws have become my reference tools as I conduct other experiments on cosmic energy.

Due to my limited resources, I can only share my thoughts about fifteen of its hexagrams. With the step-by-step procedure for reading the *I Ching* that I have introduced in this book and with all the laws listed for each hexagram on the appendices, readers of the *I Ching* can write essays on the field of their expertise.

The *I Ching* is a great leader; it welcomes comments and feedback!

Appendix I

Laws on Hexagrams 1–31

The Sixty-Four Hexagrams

The sixty-four hexagrams of the *I Ching* are globally recognized as the codes of natural law. Each hexagram, given in the correct order the name of each (in the context of Chinese characters) identifies its role in the growth process. The translated English names of the hexagrams, regrettably, do not carry such connotations.

These hexagrams are grouped in the *I Ching* in two parts representing two different phases of sociopolitical development. Hexagrams one through thirty express the evolution of sociopolitical economic organizations; hexagrams thirty-one through sixty-four express the evolution of social order, primarily the institute of family and related matters.

The laws of each hexagram are shown in italics, while my explanations are in regular print.

1 Chien-乾
Yang Force

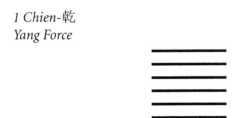

This is the only hexagram with all yang lines, contrary to the core theme of the *I Ching*, which usually shows yin and yang forces interacting. It illustrates the nature of the yang force in various situations and gives the laws for success when using only one force—the yang force—and the consequences. The lines represent six scenarios of the yang force at work.

Occasional, extreme circumstances could dictate the use of only one force when taking an immediate, decisive action. *Chien* addresses the various scenarios and the strategy for achieving the goal at such circumstances.

Both trigrams are metal. A sharp, penetrating vision and iron will are necessary to succeed with only one force. The act is for the exceptional person, someone possessing the strength of a dragon. As a most versatile creature, a dragon thrives equally well in water, on land, and in the sky; it swims, crawls, and flies.

Here are the laws/scenarios of using all yang force:

- *Take great patience; long, hard work is needed to fully prepare for the move.* You can't afford an error, as no opposite force provides a counterpoint to forewarn you about the shortfalls. Line one is a yang line, low and without support. This person has little experience and no help.

- *As you are prudent enough to advance to a safe spot at the right time, seek help and investigate the opportunity to make the next move forward.* It is a yang line in a yin position, without bonding help above. But being centered and protected, you are in the right mind, and you are safe to move around but not to advance too far.

- *As you move to the outer edge of your home front, stay vigilant. You should take notes of the people and the surroundings; sharpen your vision and polish your skills before you enter the new territory.* Line three is the top line of the lower (home) trigram, exposed to foreign attacks.

- *As you reach a new territory, look around before making a move. You have achieved a temporary victory to land a new job over the long haul. Now you are closer to the supreme leader, the king on line five; watch for the optimal time to make another move.* Line four is close to line five, the king, and needs to impress the king with a faultless performance to gain full approval and recognition.

- *As you become the great leader, take time to get the best help and delegate your responsibilities.* Line five, a yang line in the right position, is confident and able to make the proper decision to seek help.

- *As you are established ion the top job, share your power with top aides, carefully groom a few potential successors, and, most importantly, refrain from alienating your staff. That would be a great misfortune, as there is no support.* Line six is at the top, like the dragon going high into the sky where the air is thin; he is vulnerable to faint and fall. It is a lonely spot where few can survive.

Divination: You are likely to succeed in what you are doing or are planning to do. However, you have to be up front and practice fair play. Northwest is the good direction.

*2 Kun_*坤
Yin Force

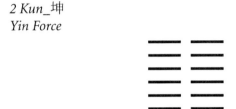

In contrast to *Chien, Kun* is a yin force. It represents the earth, the element of a dependent, a follower, or an assistant.

The hexagram explains the nature of the yin force, a persistently subtle force. With its homogeneous yin lines, the *Kun* illustrates the process and consequences of acting on yin force alone, typically as a helpless and faithful dependent under the total care of a great provider.

It is the best life. However, there is a price to pay. The *Kun* hexagram illustrates the nature of such a force, the strategy to play, and the consequence of using extreme yin force to succeed in a supporting role.

- *Be extremely observant and perceptive of your surroundings, the people included, especially those having power over you; take notes and take precautions. Anticipate freezing weather when you see frost, and prepare for the coming snow.* Anticipate your fate, and accommodate whatever comes along without grievances. Shovel the snow, and walk on the ice if you have to. Line one is lowly and humble with no bonding help and in the wrong position. She is at the mercy of her leaders.

- *Be honest, sincere, fair, and forgiving in your dealings with others.* Line two is a yin line in the right position and is protected. By being observant and patient, she has advanced to a right position, and she can gracefully enjoy the blessing.

- *Be subtle in your approach to reach a goal. Hide your objective from the interest of your provider as long as it takes. Your talent will surface in due time.* Line three has advanced to the edge, planning to leap to a higher position, the wrong position, and he is unprotected and not centered. When you are not in your most favorable circumstance and not protected, you have to hide, regardless of your great talent.

- *Keep your ambition to yourself when you are not in a position to fulfill it. Tie up your belt, and keep your lips tight.* Line four has succeeded in establishing itself in a new front but remains on the first line of the outer trigram. This person is in her right mind but in a low, risky position. She has to remain discrete.

- *Practice modesty, and be absolutely fair with your peers when you are in a high position if you can't fully take charge.* Line five is in the king position, centered and protected, but (as a yin line) it is not strong enough to take charge of the job.

- *Prepare for war, and pay the consequence if you persistently advance without regard to the interest of your provider. When the bottled-up yin force explodes to and starts a battle with the yang force, the consequence is disastrous.* Line six finally reaches the top position, the right position, but it is not protected. If this person decides to rebel, her opponents will knock her down.

Divination: Take a supporting role, and let things go on a natural course. Enjoy good provisions, and be gracious.

Starting from the third hexagram, we can see how yin and yang forces interact in different situations.

3 *Chun*
Sprouting

This hexagram is discussed in the text.

Divination: Patience and courage are the keys to survival. The yang line at the bottom indicates the strong will to move forward but little progress over a prolonged period (three yin lines in a row).

4 Mung
Learning

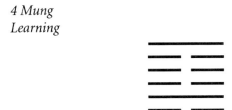

This hexagram is discussed in the text.

Divination: You are better off circulating, patiently seeking good advice and sound help; your mentality at this point is not likely to help you make sound decisions.

5 Hsu 需
Peer Competition

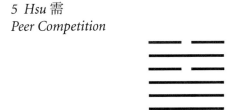

Hsu in Chinese means two things: (1) making a living and (2) moving at the right time to go after your needs.

The hexagram is about young people competing for their livelihoods. Among the trigrams is a father at home guiding two young daughters and a young son. The elements are water and metal, interbreeding.

The hexagram is about making a living with determination and prudence.

- *Watch carefully for the right timing, and keep a distance from the battlefield before you proceed.* Line one is a yang line in a right position; he is in the right mind to make a move. He is separated from the deep water by a buffer of two more yang lines above. He is watching and learning the rules of the fight from a good distance.

- *Keep waiting patiently to gauge a proper move regardless of criticism from others who push you forward.* Line two is yang line in a yin position being criticized for doing the wrong thing, but he is centered enough to stay still.

- *When you are forced to step into the edge of the battlefield, exercise great caution for protection.* Line three has moved to a risky zone, edging toward the water (the water trigram). He has to brave the danger.

- *After you reach the river (the battlefield where you will fight for a livelihood in a hazardous zone), use yin force (prudence) to observe and adapt. Do not confront a danger or an opponent.* Line four is at the unprotected edge of a foreign zone, but she is lucky enough to be a yin line in a yin position, and she knows the right thing to do.

- *As soon as you land on a good position, secure your provisions, and stay centered; do not relax.* Line five is a yang line in a yang position, protected and centered; he achieved his goal, but he knows to stay prudent.

- *When unforeseeable circumstances put you into deep water, entertain (with good food) your invading opponents for help and approval.* Line six is trapped in dangerous waters; however, as a yin line in a yin position, she can adapt in this dangerous environment. She entertains the three yang lines from afar, turning the invasion into help.

Divination: You need to proceed with caution and prudence. Listen, observe, and seek guidance from the elderly wise. Don't try to start big projects or expect great rewards.

6 *Sung* 訟
Litigation

The Chinese character of the hexagram means "verbal fight in the justice court." The two trigrams are in reverse order of the *Hsu*. Relentless competition for limited goods in the society creates litigation. This hexagram is about how to conduct litigation.

The trigrams show a mature male on top (yang lines, the *Chien* trigram symbolizing the rank of father, typically the judge) trying to resolve the conflicts among young adults of different genders and ages, represented by the trigrams of the first and middle daughters and the middle son.

Yang lines at the top indicate strong will, courage, and confidence in the fight for one's fair share; conceal your strategy with heavy cover (three solid lines piled up as a team) in the fight. Yin lines at the lower (inner) trigram indicate the wisdom of water, which is fathomless, fluid, and changeable. There are different levels of mental strategy; the yin lines are separated by a yang line, meaning you should conceal your motive and strategy all the way.

- *Find a simple way to settle a dispute. Do not let a litigation case drag on.* Line one encounters some dispute (a yin line in a yang position); while bonding to line four, it seeks a distant, reliable bond to settle the case.

- *Flee to a remote village to avoid the litigation if you have committed a fault. You have to pay for an error. Never fight a losing litigation.* Line two, a yang line, sits on a yin position, a wrong position, without bonding help. He is at fault and has no chance to win. He should hide in a remote village.

- *Having a good reason to litigate does not entitle you to a victory. Retreat to lead a quiet life if you can't afford the cost of litigation.* Line three is a yin line in a yang position, edgy, shaky, and lacking resources to fight; the bonding help at line six might not be stable enough for a sure win.

- *Withdrawing a case that you have no means to win will bring you good fortune. Reevaluate your case, and follow natural laws.* Line four is a yang line in the wrong position and is trying to bond with line one, an attempt to reconcile with an old friend.

- *When you have a justified case and are protected (guaranteed to win), and when you are resourceful enough to handle the case, go all the way to pursue your case. It would be good fortune.* Line five is properly on the high position, centered and protected; he is resourceful enough to win the fight.

- *Winning an unjustified case via foul play or improper power will put you in a shaky position and subject you to repeated punishments. If you are lucky enough to get away with it, it will be a lifetime insult for you.* Line six is a yang line in a yin position (indicating the wrong cause) with bonding help. He is likely to succeed if he uses unfair tactics. However, he might have to pay the consequences eventually.

Divination: Expect arguments, disputes, or litigation. You are likely to get help. Try to stay away from it. The seeming victory may carry repercussions.

7 Shih 師
Warring

This hexagram is discussed in the text.

Divination: Expect challenges. Do not give up on solutions. You will get help and be rewarded for your hard work.

8 Pi 比
Teamwork

This hexagram is discussed in the text.

Divination: You are likely to win cooperation from associates or family members. Assistance is available without much effort.

9 Hsiao Chu 小畜
Small Saving

Economic growth from effective team work (as shown in the *Pi* hexagram) leads to the accumulation of moderate wealth. The scenario of the trigrams depict a cloudy sky (the sun trigram is trapped inside as wind blows from outside) without rain. Small obstacles hamper great progress as one tries to move forward.

The theme of the hexagram is achieving savings by moving forward with small capital.

- *Proceed confidently on your way to financial achievements with small capital and move forward; it does not hurt to try. You can always return to the homeland if things do not work out, as you are only taking a small risk.* Line one is yang line at the right position with bonding help above. However, line four, a yin line, does not help much. The *I Ching* advises moving forward regardless of small, anticipated concerns.

- *Team with likeminded buddies, stay centered, and act properly; you will conquer the obstacles.* Line two is a yang at the yin position without bonding help, but he is cautious and prudent and has good friends all around; he could succeed with well-planned teamwork.

- *Break away from a wrong partnership when it becomes a roadblock to your progress.* Line three is a yang line in the right position, at a dangerous edge, and without bonding help; he might fall into the trap of line four, a yin. The partnership could stop him from moving to line five.

- *Remain flexible, sincere, and accommodating to your neighbors; you will get help from them to conquer the obstacles.* Line four, the only yin among five yang lines, is feeling out of place, but her open mind and accommodating attitudes are attracting the friendship from above. A yang line tends to bond to yin line.

- *You will get help by taking the first move to help your neighbors.* Line five, a yang line at the high and powerful position, is gaining the support of line four by helping a needy neighbor.

- *Know when to stop. Don't fall into the trap of greed.* Line six, a yang in a yin position, is at high risk.

Divination: Expect small gains. Exercise patience and hard work. The time is not ripe for a big success.

10 Lu 履
Propriety

The character for this hexagram means "treading the right track" (i.e., following the rules on propriety). Due to increasing confusion among various groups and teams competing for financial gain and the need to protect accumulated wealth, rules are needed to regulate conduct in society.

On top of the hexagram is the father setting rules on propriety for his three daughters. Among the six lines, only line five is in the right position, representing the qualified authority on propriety guiding a straying group. The theme is following the rules of propriety to advance to a high position.

- *Take a stand on propriety; do the right thing regardless of what others are doing.* Line one is a yang line in a yang position, not bonded to any line, separated from the yin line by line two; it is not swayed by anyone else.

- *Retreat from the group not complying with propriety, when necessary, to keep yourself clean.* Line two is tempted to mix with the yin line above (an improper bond). His option is to detach from the group.

- *Know your strength and position before picking a route of propriety for advancement. A wrong move would not succeed, and it could cost you.* Line three, the only yin in the group, is at the dangerous edge in a wrong position and without bonding support above; she is persistently pressing the great leader (the *Chien* trigram) above for a position. She does not belong to the group, so she would not be accepted. She is putting herself in an embarrassingly dangerous position.

- *As a new member edging into a powerful club, play yin force to get accepted.* Line four, a yang line in a yin position, has moved to the edge of a powerful club; he is bending to take a low position while observing how the propriety is accepted.

- *As you reach the top position, do not abuse the power of propriety; it is dangerous.* Line five, a yang line in a yang position, has no supporting yin line bonding to him.

- *Be sensitive to the results of an act of propriety. Practicing propriety is a subtle matter involving substantial gray areas. There are rules but not laws. The effectiveness of propriety is defined by the results.* Line six, a yang line in a yin position, is trying to justify his position.

Divination: Follow common sense; apply fair play and use yin force to solve your problems.

11 *Tai* 泰
Prosperity

This hexagram is discussed in the text.

Divination: You are likely to enjoy happy sailing on your life path. On the other hand, you should be content and caring, and, above all, play fair to stay prosperous.

12 P'I 否
Obstruction

```
━━━━━━━━━━
━━━━━━━━━━
━━━━━━━━━━
━━━   ━━━
━━━   ━━━
━━━   ━━━
```

Prolonged and excessive prosperity lead to greed and obsession, creating income gaps, poverty, and communication difficulty among people. The result is stagnation.

P'I in Chinese indicates setbacks, disappointments, conflicts, and misfortune in general. These two trigrams, with their contrasting natures, are placed in their natural order. The more powerful yang trigram is enjoying its natural privilege, with an upper hand over the weaker yin trigram. The disadvantaged members of society are trapped in the same rut and struggling without help; they are blocked from pushing ahead.

When society does not provide help for the disadvantaged to compete equally, it creates misfortune. When the lowly are provided with the opportunity to reach higher ground (like the *Tai*, with a yin trigram on the upper territory), prosperity abounds. We are seeing this brutal reality more in our chaotic society.

What does one do when trapped in the economic pothole of poverty? Here is the procedure:

- *Never struggle alone. Join with the right people to make a breakthrough.* Line one is a yin line in a yang position and connected with two more yin lines above. She has a team, and the group is ready for a fight. Unfortunately, her bonding help at line four is glued to the other two yang lines and is working as a powerful opponent, betraying and abandoning her.

- *Bravely and graciously accept your doomed fate for the moment; stay prudent, and work out a strategy for survival.* Line two is centered and protected; the person is prepared to plan the right move.

- *Do not put yourself into a spot vulnerable to a full attack from your opponents.* Line three edges forward to the border of the group of yang lines (representing her opponents), exposing her to the danger of the powerful attacks. She is inviting insult and trouble.

- *When reaching higher ground (making progress and getting out of a rut), look around and unite with supporters and time your actions. Keep moving forward.* Line four has reached the edge of the powerful club; on the edge but in a wrong position, he is not ready to make a change for his people. He tries to bond with line one and waits for the right time.

- *After successfully reaching a high position, carefully assess your strength and power, search for allies, and stay alert of unforeseeable traps around you.* Line five is in the king position, centered and protected, and bonded to the natural support in line two, but he is sitting between two powerful nonbonding groups, threatening his survival.

- *With perseverance, hard work, and joint efforts, we will achieve our goal.* Line six, a yang line at the yin position, represents a brave and wise person with great support who will finally succeed.

Divination: The *P'I* hexagram leads to success. Having divined the *P'I*, expect sweet fruit after a bitter struggle. Change is a typical theme throughout the *I Ching*.

13 *Tung Jen* 同人
Fellowship

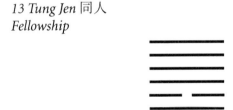

This hexagram is discussed in the text.

Divination: Expect great cooperation from associates and family, and enjoy a spirit of happy partnership. It is a wonderful time to form joint ventures. In fact, joint venture has become the most amicable avenue for succeeding at such times.

14 Ta Yu 大有
Great Possession

This hexagram is discussed in the text.

Divination: Expect great financial success. Great possessions could create undesirable effects, as all great wealth does. As a safeguard against evil, curtail the desire to possess wealth, and try to open up new fronts beyond your local community.

15 Chien 謙
Open-mindedness

Success breeds confidence, broadens vision, and invites envy from peers. The ancient Chinese valued modesty as a social self-defense, believing that truly great people were prudent enough to avoid envy from their peers.

The bottom line is that modesty is cultivated and used as a natural self-defense. Prudent people are aware of deficiencies in certain areas of their lives; they should try hard to make up for them. The goal is holistic wellness in whatever we do.

Chien illustrates the nature and function of modesty and its limitations.

- *To be modest and open-minded is to achieve inner strength and harmony. With harmony and inner strength, an individual can go through all dangers and difficult times.* Line one is lowly and yin, the wrong position. Without bonding support, it is feeble. We must work hard to identify the prerequisites for enhancing our qualities.

- *Your goal to achieve harmony has to come from your own awareness, need, and effort; it is not for vanity to put on a show.* Line two is centered, protected, and at the right position. These are the conditions for achieving harmony.

- *Great men who are silent about their great work and stay low will win the heart of the public.* Line three is the only great leader in the group, and he is shouldering all the hard work and staying on the front line to protect the people. All the yin lines are trying to bond to him, like streams traveling from high mountains to low land and flowing into the ocean.

- *Modesty and prudence go a long way.* Line four, is a yin line in the right position and doing the right thing. She can stay in a higher position even though she is less capable than line three.

- *Modesty has limitations. There are times when military force has to replace modesty.* Line five, a yin at the king position, is in the wrong position but is centered and protected. She knows how to apply physical force to maintain her great leadership.

- *Modesty has to be backed up with physical force in public leadership.* A country needs both military force and diplomacy to defend against foreign attacks.

Divination: Your project begins modestly; it will gradually progress toward great success. However, you need to proceed with an open mind. Most importantly, you must learn from evolved individuals.

16 Yu
Provisions 豫

All good things (wealth, fame, high achievement, propriety, and harmony) have created a wonderful life with abundant provisions.

In the four trigrams, three grown sons provide for the mother, with the oldest son on the top leading the younger brothers. All are united as a good team. That creates good fortune.

Here are the laws for handling good fortune:

- *Do not take your provisions for granted; do not boast about them. This will invite misfortune.* Line one is a yin line in the wrong position, lowly and unprotected; she is emboldened by bonding help from line four, and she is boasting of her good fortune. This invites misfortune.

- *Stay centered while you enjoy your great provisions. Never indulge.* Line two is a yin in the right position, centered and protected; it is the only yin line doing the right thing. The other yin lines are indulging on the provisions.

- *Restrain from greed to team up with the more powerful in foul play. It will cause regret.* Line three, a yin line advancing to the edge, is attempting to bond to line four, the only yang line, for more gain. It is risky, as they are not a natural team.

- *When being entrusted with wealth and provisions, show your integrity to attract good people to help.* Line four, the only yang line, sits in a yin position. An assistant with integrity entrusted by the king is mixing with his staff and working toward one goal.

- *Keep a watchful eye on a vicious, powerful neighbor, and keep your wealth with a good strategy. That is, stay centered.* Line five, a feeble yin line, sits on a wrong position and is vulnerable to attacks from the strong neighbor at line four, a yang line. But she is centered and protected. Use your head and seek protection.

- *Watch out constantly for changes, and take necessary steps to keep your wealth intact.* Line six is at the top and due for a change. Plan for a soft landing.

Divination: You are likely to make great, positive changes, such as moving to new territories, physically or emotionally. In any event, you are positioned to gain. Expect change and involuntary movement. Trying to cut corners will invite misfortune.

17 Sui 隨
Immigration

Sui means "following someone" or "being attracted to some new places." A prospering society with great provisions attracts newcomers from neighboring areas. Both trigrams have yang lines at the base and yin lines on the top, indicating open channels to attract a new population.

People in the trigrams are young couples with young children. A young father holds the young son, and a young mother holds the young daughter; they are typical immigrants.

Sui elaborates on the principles of adjusting to a new society. Follow these steps to establish your livelihood in a new home:

- *On arrival, get out of the house to look for jobs and do what the Romans are doing, but stay honest.* Line one is yang line in the yang position, low and with no bonding help. Work hard to be self-reliant when making a fresh start; obey the law (and stay in the right position).

- *As you slowly settle down, look for improvements, and go the extra mile to get a better job.* Line two is bonded to line five above. But she is tempted to bond with line one below for convenience. That is a dangerous move. Bond to good and powerful people to better your life.

- *Make a proper choice between the good and the powerful when looking for a boss (or supporter). There is risk in serving the powerful, but there is also something to gain.* Line three has advanced to the edge of leaving her job; she is tempted to bond to the yang line above and abandon her old boss at home. Exercise prudence.

- *As your advancement threatens your superior, be open and honest, staying on good terms in the relationship.* Line four, a yang line, is threatening to take over the position of line five; he has to be sensitive and honest in every move.

- *When in charge of a team or an organization, play fair and team up with the good and fair subordinates far and near.* Line five is a yang line in the right position, centered and protected. This is a perfect scenario for a great leader.

- *Playing honestly will bond you to strong, good providers/supporters.* Line six, a yin line in the highest right position, is bonded to both lines five and four because she is doing the right thing.

Divination: Expect good leads when changing jobs or relocating. Take a humble approach when beginning a new life. You will advance by playing honestly.

> *18 Kui* 蠱
> *Decay*

The Chinese name of the hexagram means "worms in a can," referring to decayed or spoiled food in a container. This symbolizes corruption at the top.

The scenario is wind trapped within a mountain, symbolizing isolation and separation; in short, pockets of decay have been created by the predecessors (the two yin lines on the top trigram). This has to be corrected by the younger people below. Here are the steps to correcting corruption:

- *Correcting corruption takes hard work; it takes energetic young people with new ideas to catch the decay before it advances too far.* Line one, a yin line in the wrong position, is weak without bonding help. She has to stop the decay from spreading.

- *Waste no time blaming your predecessors; do the right thing.* Line two is a yang line (the able son of the mother at line five, both bonded) at the yin position (using his mental skill); he is centered and protected. He will do the right thing with his strength.

- *Make the change smooth on your predecessors or parents.* Line three, a yang line at the yang position, approaches the edge; he is properly pushing his way to the outer zone to correct the corruption.

- *Make the change thorough; do not take excuses from someone while changing course.* Line four is a yang line in the yin position, implying that a combination of physical and mental strength is needed to implement the project.

- *Hire the capable to implement the change.* Line five, a yin, is centered and protected but not in the right position. She is bonding to the yang line above for help to overcome her weakness.

- *If the corrupted state is too deep-rooted to allow any change, detach yourself from the politics; hold on to the principle of reform, and spread the seeds by teaching or writing.* Line six is a yin line on the top, using the highest mental power to bond with powerful people to make a change.

Divination: Expect big cleansing from the newcomers. Older individuals must open new channels of communication. It is time for soul-searching and finding solutions.

19 Lin 臨
New Leadership

Lin means "to get close to." Leaders should connect with and show concern for the people. Hexagrams nineteen through twenty-one offer an integrated program for correcting corruption.

Lin represents thunder breaking ground and clamoring for attention. The thunder trigram at the middle is moving through the earth trigram above. It also represents thunder over a pond, causing more splashes.

Yin lines far outnumber yang lines, so the approach requires wisdom more than physical power. Yang lines push forward to the yin lines, correcting the corruption along the way.

Here is the strategy for building new leadership:

- *Start with the right leader. The character of the leader is the key to sending the most powerful message.* Line one, a yang in the right position, is honest and up front; he is entrusted by the higher-ups, as he is bonding correctly to line four.

- *Approach the problem with strength, determination, and the proper procedure.* Line two—centered and protected, bonding to line five, and sitting in a yang line position—is properly combining yin and yang forces to solve the problem.

- *Do not use sweet talk to cheat the people. It creates misfortune.* Line three, a yin line in a yang position without bonding help, is trying to lead the people with tricks. That will create misfortune.

- *Use right people.* Line four is nudging toward a high position and bonding to line one. When correcting corruption, involve the right people from all levels.

- *Use wisdom to delegate responsibilities.* Line five is in the king position, centered and protected and bonded to line two. Entrusts your subordinates with responsibilities.

- *Be benevolent to subordinates.* Line six, at the highest position, is mixing with all the yin lines as a group.

Divination: Find out the truth. In any event, wisdom is preferred over physical power.

20 Kuan 觀
Good Example

Kuan means "to observe." This hexagram is about how to guide the people by setting good examples, including by displaying signs and symbols. Good examples give guidance to the people (as represented by the wind trigram blowing over the earth or land).

Government officials can demonstrate good conduct, but they can also erect national symbols such as museums and libraries, show propriety in celebrations, and support the infrastructure of the country. These symbols reflect the strength of the leadership and impact the people.

Here is the strategy for displaying national symbols:

- *The symbols and conduct displayed by the leading groups have to command respect and admiration. Insignificant symbols are only for ignorant, small people. It would insult the knowledgeable people, creating a negative impact.* Line one is a yin line in the wrong position, low and without support. It has no good effect on society.

- *The symbols should be displayed openly to attract attention.* Line two is centered in the right position, bonding to yang line five, and properly attracting attention.

- *Use good judgment to evaluate and learn from such signs to make decisions. Don't be fooled by the message of the signs.* Line three is a yin line at the edge of the trigram, in a wrong position, and bonded to the top line. She is advancing away from her homefolk but is blocked from reaching her supporter by another yin line above. In this dilemma, she has to use good sense to make the right judgment.

- *As leaders of the people, we should visit different parts of the country and read the messages from all the signs to understand the people and their culture.* Line four is a yang line in a yin position, mixing with three more yin lines below, meaning he is stepping into the shoes of others.

- *The top leader should take time to study the signs in his kingdom to connect himself to his subjects.* Line five, at the king's position, is overlooking all the yin lines below, learning about the display.

- *The great leader, on the other hand, should be aware that he is being watched by his people. He needs to be a role model.* Line six is on display at the most visible position.

Divination: Expect an unsettled life. You are likely to be confronted with minor problems in various areas. Do the right thing.

21 Shih Ho 噬嗑
Punishment

Shih Ho means "breaking obstacles by closing the jaws to bite." Crime, an obstacle to a peaceful society, has to be punished and destroyed. Thus, the hexagram is about how to apply punishments.

The two fundamental trigrams are fire and thunder, symbolizing powerful law with sparkling results. Leaders should make the laws loud and clear to all subjects (like the sun and the thunder), and laws should be fair and justified and applied equally to all offenders; everyone knows what to expect, and no one is misled or wrongly convicted. The law has to be carried out with effective force, like great heat and thunder.

Here are the principles:

- *Punish small crimes as a means to stop bigger ones (i.e., starting from the toes, as the commentary indicates).* Line one is a yang at the right position, lowly but determined and correct. Punish criminals with force even when the infraction is small and insignificant.

- *Implement the punishment to induce repentance but not to damage the offender.* Line two, a yin line at the right position, is centered and protected. As an assistant of the king, she is using good sense to protect her subjects and maintain order at the same time.

- *Implement punishment with decisive force.* Line three, as a yin line in the wrong position, is at the edge, and she is in a critical position to correct wrongdoings; she bravely looks up to the yang force at line four for help.

- *Have an iron will and make arrow-sharp decisions.* Line four is a yang line in a yin position; he is combining wisdom and force and courageously overruling the king (a yin line of less strength) to apply punishment.

- *Restrain from unnecessary punishments.* Line five is a yin line at the majestic king position, the improper position. The king puts himself in the shoes of the offenders while trying to evaluate the nature of the punishments.

- *Avoiding the spread of crime is the best way to rule a country.* Line six is a yang line in a yin position using his wisdom to stop crime with his powerful strength.

Divination: *Shih Ho* represents interruption, conflict, or legal entanglements. You need to be patient and avoid shortcuts.

22 Pi 賁
Civil Grace

The excessive use of strict punishment calls for codes on civil grace to keep society in harmony.

A mountain is brightened with sunlight. The sun is shining with glamour, putting on a great show. However, because a water trigram is above, the sun's heat barely penetrates; it is not strong enough to create fundamental change. The light is, therefore, superficial and for show only.

The theme of the hexagram is educating the public on civil or social grace. Here are the codes:

- *Civil grace should match the behavior and inner quality of the person/ people/country, starting from the bottom.* Line one is yang line at the right position and bonded to line four; connecting right from the start is good.

- *Look to people of higher ability and quality as role models in practicing social grace.* Line two is centered and protected without a bonding line; she looks to line three, the yang line above, for a role model.

- *Civil grace has to be supported with quality. It should serve a proper function beyond simply exciting the people.* Line three is caught between two yin lines, but neither is a natural bonding partner; he is not admired by the appropriate people. It is not a good civil grace.

- *Plain attire is suitable in special circumstances. It is not always necessary to prepare meticulous attire. The substance of civil grace counts more.* Line four needs to bond with line one, her natural partner, but she is blocked by line three, another yang line close by. She needs to dash forward to meet her mate and has no time to dress up.

- *Dressing up is the important thing, and setting priorities should stand out as the top issue. When setting up codes on civil grace, pay attention to long-term effects.* Line five is a yin line in a yang position, without a bonding line; she is centered and visionary enough to be objective to do the right thing.

- *The ultimate goal of civil grace is to promote proper civil behavior, not just superficial mannerisms.* Line six, a yang line in the yin position, is not in the right position and not bonded to line three; instead, he is attracted by the wrong admirers from lines five and four.

Divination: You will have some success with small projects. The timing is not favorable for significant tasks.

23 Po 剝
Exfoliation

Po means "peeling off by layers." Excessive social grace and ceremonial propriety leads to vanity and senseless formality. As quality declines, the society starts to decay. The decay, however, starts from the bottom, a reversal of the *Kui.* This hexagram naturally takes a different strategy and wisdom.
Here is the procedure:

- *The decay starts from the ground, spreading to the legs of the bed.* Line one is a yin line in the wrong position; something wrong is taking place. A yin force (decay) is breaking ground, gaining a foothold, and spreading.

- *The decay has reached the bottom of the bed. There is no immediate danger yet.* Line two is centered and protected but surrounded by all yin forces; the decay will certainly continue.

- *Stop the spread by detaching from the source; team up with good people to block the decaying force.* Line three, suffering from the advancing decay, is backing away to the periphery to get help from her bonding line six on the top, the only bonding pair. To fight a spreading decay, you have to detach yourself from the source first.

- *Keep fighting the decay with full force; there is no time to consider options.* Line four is a yin line in a yin position; she has the right mind to manage the decay.

- *As a leader, line up the crowd in the decaying process, assigning each member proper responsibility.* Line five, at the climax of the decay, the last defense, has to issue an order.

- *The result of the scheme depends on the quality of the leader; a fair leader with strength (a yang force) will tame the bad guy (a yin force); the crooked (a yin force) will reinforce the decay process to the destruction of the nation/ organization.* Line six, the only yang line, is imposing the optimal force to stop the decay. Only a yang force can manage a yin force.

Divination: Shake off old, unproductive habits, and explore new ways of doing things. The time is not favorable for aggression.

24 Fu 復
Recovery

Fu can mean "back to the origin," "recovering," or "rebuilding." *Fu* is the opposite of *Po*. Recovery is the natural course of a prolonged decay. A great leader will pick up the pieces to reestablish order. Yang force will replace yin (decay).

This yang will slowly gain a foothold, pushing upward to establish itself and rebuild a healthy order. Recovery takes power—like thunder breaking in the air,—loud, clear, continuous, and decisive. Here is the procedure:

- *Target the right time. Rebuilding is a difficult task; effort must be coordinated with the Almighty. Before initiating your effort, you need to plan and wait.* Line one is a yang line in the right position with an overwhelming number of subjects longing to bond to him (all the yin lines above the only yang, representing his people seeking peace and order).

- *Gather the good people to move forward.* Line two is centered and protected, trying to team with line one for help.

- *Reforming may take trials and corrections; one should guard against committing an error.* Line three has pushed to the edge and is ready to move to the new trigram; being in wrong position, she is making and correcting errors in the process.

- *Stay with principles; return to the right path when necessary.* Line four has moved into a new zone and has discovered an error; he returns to bond to line one. The right line at the right position knows the right path to take.

- *Stay with your commitment. After you achieve your goal of recovery, keep your work going.* Line five is centered and protected on the highest position. She has reached a point of no return, and she should take the job because it is right and necessary.

- *Guard against repeating the same error of having decay in your nation, organization, or life. It would be another long, torturous process.* Line six is a yin line in the right position checking on what has happened and learning a lesson.

Divination: Look forward to a positive change or favorable recovery. Carefully check your work, and correct errors at the very beginning.

25 *Wu Wang* 旡妄
Follow the Reality

Wu means "no." *Wang* can refer to deceit, error, vanity, or wishful thinking. Together, *Wu Wang* symbolizes the reality or truth. The hexagram preaches the essence of truth.

During a slow recovery, people should learn about the truth and should begin to follow the natural course by doing things that are naturally correct. The virtues of kindness, fairness, and integrity are stressed. *Wu Wang* calls for prudence and persistence in observing natural laws.

Here are ways to follow the truth:

- *Knowing the reality and following its course serves us best.* Line one is a yang line at the right position; he understands the truth and does the right thing from the very beginning.

- *Be realistic. Your knowledge of natural timing and effort determine your harvest. Never expect a surprising harvest without cultivation. Things happen with a reason and run on a natural course.* Line two is a yin line in a right position, centered and protected, and bonded to line five; she is doing the right thing to prepare for advancement.

- *Deliberate precautions and good deeds, required for success, do not guarantee security, good return, or a good life. Misfortune is unavoidable for anyone, regardless of all measures of precaution; it is part of the natural course, just as your precious cow being secured upon a post in your shed could disappear. Unfortunately, the innocent neighbors would become victims as suspects in the theft. We need to heed this truth.* Line three is a yin line in a yang position. He is strong, healthy, and in the right mind to do the right thing, but he is at an unprotected edge and exposed to accidents. He has to prepare for misfortune and take a realistic attitude toward life.

- *Being fair will steer you from making errors.* Line four is a yang line in a yin position, bending to the truth, putting herself into the shoes of the other party, and trying to play a fair game.

- *Being truthful is the surest way to stay on track.* Line five is yang line in the right position between two other yang lines, representing honesty on all fronts.

- *Do not force issues of reality/truth to the extreme; it would put you to a dead end and misfortune. Reality is not absolute.* Line six, a yang line in a yin position, is at the top and joining with all the yang lines; the person is protecting the truth to the end without compromise. Unprotected, he is putting himself in a wrong and dangerous position.

Divination: Stay away from greed and wishful thinking. Good fortune comes with hard work and fair play.

> 26 *Ta Chu* 大畜
> *Great Accumulation*

Ta means "big," and *Chu* means "hoarding/accumulating." A realistic approach and attitude leads to the accumulation of wealth or power. *Ta Chu* is to accumulate the required power or knowledge to fulfill a goal.

The theme is cultivating strength for the big job. Here are the laws:

- *Avoid crossing a risk zone when you have not accumulated enough strength for the job.* Line one is yang line in the right position with bonding help on line four, a tempting scenario. However, being at the low position with two more yang lines above trying to bond with line four, he is prudent enough not to cross the barrier.

- *Use prudence to resist the temptation of premature advancement.* Line two has impressed a higher-up with his hard work and is offered a great job by line five (his bonding help). However, he realizes that he is not ready for the post. He is at the right position and centered enough to conquer the temptation of crossing the barrier of line three.

- *Think twice when you are ready to make a decisive move; be fully prepared for a sudden, mandatory retreat if necessary.* Line three has advanced to the edge of his homeland, but there is no bonding help ahead; he might be able to cross the two yin lines, but it is not a sure bet.

- *If you anticipate a necessary retreat in your advancement, start it as soon as possible.* Line four is a yin line in a right position with bonding help back home. She should do the right thing.

- *Upon the encroaching threat against your advancement, do not directly confront it; trace the origin of the threat, and try to eliminate it.* Line five has reached the king position and is feeling the threat from line six to undo her power. Being a yin line, centered and protected, she should use yin force for protection.

- *The most effective way to deal with threat is to channel it in divergent directions.* Line six is a yang line on the top in a yin position, the wrong position, so he is confronted with threats and other problems. With two yin lines offering different directions of travel, he should take note of the opportunities.

Divination: You are likely to be nervous and apprehensive and slightly resentful at times. Your project takes long-term hard work. However, after all the hard work comes great reward. A long journey is favored.

27 Yi 頤
Nourishment

This hexagram is discussed in the text.

Divination: You are likely to enjoy good entitlement and a good life. However, you must be cautious in what you eat and say or write.

28 Ta Kuo 大過
Great Crossing

This hexagram is discussed in the text.

Divination: You must dream big and be creative. To score a victory, gather all the help, yin and yang, great and small. Spring (in March, the equivalent of lunar February) is your best time to act. Wood-related projects have a better chance of success.

29 Kan 坎
Danger

Kan means "a sink hole or deep water," dangerous traps. Reckless moves to fulfill unjustified dreams lead us into deep trouble. *Kan* is a scenario of deep water; a thunder trigram is intercepted by a mountain trigram, indicating a frustrating period of dilemmas and dangers when a solution is out of sight.

How do we handle deep trouble? Two ears, one hand, and one foot appear among the four trigrams, meaning we must listen and seek advice, apply wisdom, and quietly (by subtly working with the hand and foot, symbols hidden in the trigrams) find a way out. Here is the procedure:

- *Try by all means to never get into deep water in the first place; it is always a great misfortune.* Line one is a yin line at the yang (the wrong) position without bonding help. With low ability and no help, he is committing a great misfortune, as there is no way out.

- *When the circumstance allows a rescue plan, settle with small progress and a gradual solution, one step at a time.* Line two is a yang line in a yin position with no bonding help; he is fortunate to be centered and to remain above the water. He should try to get out one step at a time.

- *When you are in deep water with no rescue in sight, try by all means to stay alive and to wait for the dust to clear.* Line three is in the deep zone between two bodies of water with no way out. Nothing can be done.

- *Be creative and persistent enough to get help. Forgo any formality.* After slowly moving toward safety, line four is closer to the shore at line five; he should use any means available to get help from a higher rank such as a king.

- *Take the optimal time to launch a safe landing.* Line five has finally reached a temporary landing site, but he is not out of the water yet. He is centered and capable, trying to find a permanent and safe landing site.

- *Getting out of extremely deep water will take years of suffering.* Line six is a yin line in a yin position without bonding help. It will take her a long time to find the safe landing site.

Divination: Keep calm in your difficult state. Go slow, get help, and plan a logical exit.

30 Li
Radiance

This hexagram is discussed in the text.

Divination: Expect relief from current stress; help is on the horizon. However, it is not a good time to develop intimate relationships. Always keep a distance from those around you. Caution is demanded.

The *Li* hexagram concludes the first phase of the evolution of the human institute.

Appendix II

Laws on Hexagrams 31–64

Hexagram thirty-one starts another phase of the social process in the *I Ching's* themes: the evolution of social order. It starts with the process of dating, the beginning of a family. Free dating among young people was practiced at the time of the *I Ching* before rules of propriety were established.

31 Hsien 咸
Dating

This hexagram is discussed in the text.

Divination: *Hsien* means "the possibility of upcoming good fortune," such as financial gain or the fulfillment of a goal, migration to a foreign land, or a positive change. The fortunate direction of the move would be to the southwest (the opposite of the direction in the *Ken* trigram, northeast of the young boy) whether for the pleasant location or to find a potential mate.

32 Heng 恆
Marriage

This hexagram is discussed in the text.

Divination: Expect smooth and steady progress and good companionship. However, be apprehensive about change and make adjustments.

33 Tun 遯
Retreat

Reality dictates that we need to retreat from some threatening situations for self-protection. The *I Ching* suggests retreat as a means to recuperate from a damaging or dangerous relationship.

The trigrams in the hexagram include the oldest daughter, a young boy, and a father (two trigrams) but no mother or wife; the key link is missing. The group's relationships are confusing; the father is performing a role as a caretaker like a mother and a breadwinner as well. In ancient China, husbands always kept the children after the dissolution of a marriage.

The scenario also refers to a corrupted and dangerous state threatening good people to retreat. The *I Ching* recommends a decisive retreat in the face of danger. The way to win over a yang force is by yin force (i.e., going the other way, or retreating).

Here is the procedure:

- *In anticipation of danger, try to be the first one to leave.* As a yin line in a yang position, line one apprehends the danger, looks up for bonding help, and searches for an exit.

- *Stay calm for temporary protection; exit in the proper circumstance to get the right help.* Line two is centered and protected and bonded to line five for external help.

- *As you exit to a new territory, do not look back. Don't let any of your precious attachments or possessions delay your retreat.* Line three has inched to the periphery, abandoning the two yang lines behind him.

- *After arriving at a safe zone, forget your bond at home and try hard to stay in safety.* Line four is the front line of the foreign land, but it naturally bonds to line one in the homeland. He has to look forward.

- *After establishing yourself in a safe zone, you may bond to your homeland and to those you love and have left behind, if possible, but do not jeopardize your position for that matter. Your folks at home would understand.* Line five has reached far and high; he is centered, protected, and in the right position. He can use good judgment to help the loved ones behind him.

- *Get used to the new territory and its lifestyle. Make a recovery plan, or be happy about it.* Line six has reached the most remote zone without a partner.

Divination: Your setback is temporary; you will see results after long, hard work. Success will occur between the years (or months or days) of the horse and the ox, a period of seven years (or seven months or seven days, depending on the timeframe). All your miseries will disappear eventually. Meanwhile, watch out for the bad guys.

34 Ta Chuang 大壯
Expansion

Retreat has to be temporary. After sufficient recuperation, plan a comeback. This hexagram is the reversal of retreat: two yin lines are at the top, and four yang lines are at the bottom. The person is gaining strength and returning to the home front. The father is leading the young—the third daughter and the oldest son. Here are the laws to follow when launching a comeback:

- *A strong big toe does not guarantee a victory. Plan and move with caution. You need good timing and bonded support to succeed.* Line one is a yang line in the right position, strong and rightful but without bonding help. Physical strength alone is not enough to achieve great things.

- *Move at the right time and in the right place, with bonding help.* Line two is centered and protected with bonding help from line five above.

- *As your action gains momentum and you are out of your protected zone, move with caution.* Line three is a yang line at the right but risky position; he is separated from his bonding help at line six by another yang line at line four, and he is in danger of being caught.

- *Your action is gaining ground in a foreign territory; it is time to move forward with full force.* Line four is at the top of four yang lines united in a row without interruption, ready to take over the two yin lines ahead. It is time to move forward with full force.

- *After the victory, your forward-going momentum begins to decline. Take time to reflect and manage your new life. This is not the time to launch another big action.* It is a yin line in a yang position, centered, high, and protected but in the wrong position (in the wrong place at the wrong time). Big action does not continue forever. Prepare for a setback.

- *When the setback continues, don't get caught; be patient to avoid further disasters. Prudence pays off.* Line six has reached the powerful barrier; she is prudent enough to stop.

Divination: The time is right for big action, but you need to get help to succeed. The right time is the rabbit year, month, or day (depending on the timeframe and nature of your action plan), and the direction for seeking help or launching the action is the east. Watch out for unexpected setbacks and interruptions.

35 Chin 晉
Advancing

Chin means reporting to the emperor on your good work as an official in a local town. As the king sits in the north (the great king position in metaphysics), subordinates start from the southeast or southwest and report to the boss.

Good workers will be rewarded with promotions or materials, depending on their job evaluations or report cards. Here are the procedures on reporting to the boss:

- *On your first job, if your hard work did not produce a good report card, and if you don't have the right help in the government to commend you, feel comfortable to report anyway. You can do better next time.* Line one, humble and lowly, is a yin line in a yang position (meaning he is not performing well). His bonding mate, line four, is a yang line in the wrong position and unable to offer proper help. He goes forward with the evaluation anyway.

- *When you did every thing right to manage a good report card, but there is no one in the government to help you, do not let it be your concern; just do what you have to do. You will be rewarded eventually from other sources, if not from the king.* Line two is a yin line at the right position, centered and protected, without bonding help from line five; he is confidently moving forward.

- *With great support from your hometown on your good work, you can afford the risk of asking for a promotion.* Line three, a yin line in a yang position, is taking the risk to make a change. With bonding help above and the support of like minded people at home (three yin lines in one group, symbolizing full support for one mind and one goal), he has a good chance to succeed.

- *If you use dishonest tactics to move up and have reached a high position, handle the shaky position with caution.* Line four, a yang line in a yin position, has moved to the high position by improper means; At the edge of the outer trigram, exposed to danger.

- *If you got the top job with honesty and good work, try your best to always do the right thing. Don't be concerned about your capacity to perform. You will continue to make progress and eventually prove yourself to the boss.* A yin line is in a yang position, the improper position, but centered and protected.

- *When you have reached a position of extreme power overlooking many departments and districts, handle the power with great care. A vital error would cost you your career; you need to go through a new process to rebuild it.* A yang line is in a wrong position at a dangerously high point. The only path leads downward. This calls for great caution.

Divination: *Chin* indicates good fortune, financial gain, fame, and good position. Expect good news repeatedly from your subordinates or as a result of your past efforts. The auspicious time is the closing of the rat year or the beginning of the ox year (or the corresponding months/days, depending on the timeframe of your action plan).

36 Ming I 明夷
Getting Hurt

Unchecked, upward movement creates envy and resentment from others, eventually inviting attacks. The person gets hurt. How does a person avoid this fate and handle the consequences? This hexagram instructs you to hide your brilliant talent (represented by the sun, or Li, trigram) behind the gentle and docile appearance of a cow (symbolized in the *Kun* trigram as a quiet, hardworking ox). The light trigram (a symbol of brilliant talent) is placed beneath the earth trigram. Keep your spirit up and your mind bright while deceptively putting on a docile look. Below are the laws:

- *At the first sight of a coming attack, flee like a bird, abandoning your position and belongings.* A yang line in yang position symbolizes an able person in the right frame of mind to make immediate decisions.

- *After the first attack (when you failed to flee ahead), get help (from a horse, or any logistic media) and flee as soon as possible.* Line two is a yin line at the right position, protected by two yang lines; the person may be weak but can manage an escape with the proper support.

- *With a bad wound (after an attacked), you need special tactics. As your life is in danger, you need a long-term plan for protection. A revolution or counterattack is in the picture. Whatever the situation, hide safely first.* A yang line in the right position is at risk at the edge of the lower trigram. The person, however, is brave and knows to look for a safe spot.

- *Your hiding place should never be your home, the home of your clan, or any place nearby. However, try to mix with the crowd.* Line four is in a new territory (away from the homeland). It is A yin line in a yin position (representing the right hiding spot) mixing with the crowd (the three consecutive yin lines).

- *At the new place, disguise yourself, pick up a lowly job, and mix with the crowd. Keep your heart and spirit up.* We see a yin line in a yang position, the wrong position, but it is centered and protected. The displaced person is correctly staying in a safe spot.

- *The extreme hardship will disappear, just as the sun returns after the dark night.* Line six is at the end of the hiding game and ready for a change after returning to the sun trigram below. All hardship will end with time and the right circumstance.

Divination: Stay away from the battlefield; wait until the timing is right for a comeback. Progress a*nd solutions are on the horizon. The critical period consists of the months or years between the tiger and the snake.

37 Chia Jen 家人
Managing a Family

```
═══════════
═══   ═══
═══════════
═══   ═══
═══════════
═══════════
```

This hexagram is discussed in the text.

Divination: It is a fortunate hexagram for divination. All troubles have turned out to be blessings in disguise. Great news and helpful people are coming your way. The best time for realizing blessings is late spring. Your sons (or any of your children) will do very well.

38 Kuie 睽
Polarizing

```
═══════════
═══   ═══
═══════════
═══   ═══
═══════════
═══════════
```

Kuie means "not looking at each other eye to eye." The two trigrams, water and metal, make conflicting teammates. Conflicting interests take place in a small social unit such as a family and even more so in a society.

How do we live with differences and contrarians and make the best of the situation? This hexagram offers a strategy for different scenarios. Among the four trigrams, the people are a young daughter and two middle daughters separated by a middle son; no parents or elder siblings lead or guide the children. The children go astray and misbehave. The two sun trigrams mingled with the river and the lake; they are not shining and not looking at each other. Here is how to iron out the differences:

- *Differences are a part of life. Learn from the contrarians to broaden your visions and view the world from different perspectives. Even the saint returned a visit to a corrupted government official.* Line one is not getting help from line four because they are not bonded. However, he moves to line two (a yang line) regardless of the indifference of his partner.

- *Seek help from some obscure source if you fail in the regular channel. Do not assume your entitled help always comes from the same channel. Try to look into a small alley.* Lines two and five are openly bonded, but line two has found a partner at line three, representing a short and broken alley hidden between two big roads (the two yang lines).

- *Initial difference between two bonded partners might cause obstacles in their reunion; with effort and determination from both, they should iron out the difference and compromise.* Lines three and six are bonded, but both are in the wrong positions. Line three is blocked by another yang line from moving forward, while line six is pulled away from line three by another yin line (a woman). They need to iron out the deviance.

- *Use mutual trust to work out differences when there is no natural bond between the parties.* Lines four and one are both yang lines with great integrity and can trust each other regardless of the lack of a bond.

- *Focus on the power of a natural bond to smooth differences if you don't have the strength or position to do so.* Line five is a yin line (weaker than a yang line) in a wrong position but bonded to line two. Unity is power.

- *Remove the blockage of doubt between you and your partner. Show your trust.* Line six is bonded to line three (forming a natural pair of yin and yang lines); however, another yin line is closer to line six, and another yang line is closer to line three; both try to destroy the bond. Partners have to overcome these obstacles.

Divination: You will have no peace of mind while struggling to pick up the pieces. Financial loss is imminent. Expect unpleasant things and news to come your way, but none will bring significant harm. You need to spend time to fix the situation and restore the harmony.

39 Chien 蹇
Limping

―― ――
―― ――
――――――
―― ――
――――――
―― ――

This hexagram is discussed in the text.

Divination: Search your soul and find on the proper solutions to your problems. Look to the southwest, the mature female, for help. You will find good help in the confusion. The goat days, months, or years are the promising times.

40 Hsieh 解
Releasing

―― ――
――――――
―― ――
――――――
―― ――
―― ――

The components of the Chinese character for this hexagram represent cutting something off with a knife. *Hsieh* literally means "untying a knot," "melting down," "forgiving," or "finding solutions for difficulties."

With the *Chen* (foot) on the top and *Kan* (eye, water) below, the hexagram implies planning a strategy to walk out of the dangerous water. From the connotations of the trigrams, thunder from the sky is turning into water on the ground. Solving a problem takes power and courage. There is no more shock or noise but rather peace for all.

Five out of the six lines in the hexagram are in wrong positions; the only line in the right position is the one at the top. The lines symbolize a problem that has been dealt with and finally corrected.

Here is the procedure for creating solutions:

- *Look for a solution at the first sight of a problem; search hard for data.* Line one sits in the wrong position, signifying the beginning of a problem. Fortunately, line four offers bonding help, and line two (as a yang line) inspires different ideas and perspectives for creating solutions.

- *Face the problem squarely and troubleshoot all the problem spots one by one with direct, sharp effort.* Line two is a yang line in a wrong position, confronted with yin lines on both fronts. To reach his bonding help on line five, he has to win over the barrier line three, a yin line trying to bond to him; she is not a proper mate, so this is not a good solution. To reach his right mate, he has to deal with another yang line that is more accessible to line five. He is, therefore, confronted with the problems of yin and yang obstacles. He patiently shoots each troublemaker with sharp arrows.

- *Do not compound a problem with improper conduct.* Line three, a yin in a yang position, has put herself on the edge; she is not centered or protected and does not have bonding help above. She is in danger of falling off the cliff. Stay away from vanity and greed to avoid pitfalls.

- *Quickly cut off any tie with the bad guy to get the support of the good people.* Line four is in the wrong position, so he has some odds against him and some problems to solve. Unfortunately, his bonding help is also in a wrong position. Line four has to cut off this potential partner and unite with other good people.

- *Take further measures to ensure all bad guys are out of your comfort zone.* Against all odds, line five, a yin line, finally reaches the lead position and takes charge. She manages to block the bad guys (represented with a yang line below).

- *As soon as the problems are solved, immediately eliminate any approaching bad guys.* We see a yin line at the right position; the problem is solved. However, line four, a yang line in a wrong position (not a good person), is trying to bond to line six to share in the success. This person has to be eliminated.

Divination: Anticipate big, positive changes in your favor. You might lose something that you used to be fond of, but you will gain from new jobs and a new life. Progress is anticipated.

41 Sun 損
Sacrifice

Sun means "decreasing benefit," or "getting a victim to shoulder a loss." A government must sacrifice a small group of people to accomplish a goal that can benefit the majority. But it has to be done properly and fairly.

The trigrams are mountain and pond. The pond is on a lower position supporting the mountain on the top, representing the people helping the government. The theme also applies to individuals, implying that we should sacrifice present comfort for future gain. All the line pairs are bonded, indicating sacrifice made in reciprocal terms. Here are the laws:

- *Take immediate action to sacrifice for a good cause when it comes as the only option. Initiate good help from viable sources.* Line one is a yang line in a correct position, trying to bond to line four. There is good reason to impose sacrifice on any group.

- *Upon the call for sacrifice, evaluate options with the proper perspective. Search hard, and take the option that will achieve the same or better results without involving sacrifice from anyone.* Line two is centered and protected (in the right mind to make good decisions and protected from loss). It bonds to line five for a mutually benefiting cause.

- *Ask for sacrifice from the most resourceful, who can most afford it.* Line three, one of the three yin lines, stands as one of the few options. A leader has to make a good choice.

- *Implement measures quickly when sacrifice of some parties is deemed viable.* Line four, a yin line, needs immediate help from line one below.

- *A fair leader who properly taxes the resourceful to look after the needy will get support from his or her people.* Line five, a yin line, is centered and protected. It is not in the right position (not capable to provide for the subjects), but it is in the right mind to do right things.

- *When it comes to sacrifice, the super resourceful on the top should be role models, shouldering the act with their own resources.* Line six, on top of three yin lines (representing the needy), is looking after the less fortunate.

Divination: Expect losses or to be shortchanged somewhere. Good rewards will follow a difficult beginning. Take the initiative to cut costs.

42 Yi 益
Benefit

Yi can stand for increase, advancement, benefit, or compensation. After achieving results by sacrificing some group, try to properly compensate those who suffered from the sacrifice.

This hexagram is about how to give and receive help to benefit people or promote good will. Wind from the upper trigram moves down to reinforce the thunder, which sound echoes louder and farther. Both parties mutually reinforce the benefit. All lines are in bonded pairs, meaning the acts of giving and receiving work both ways.

Here are the principles of give-and-take:

- **To give:** *Giving compensation from the top (such as from the government, the well-to-do, and the powerful) to the disadvantaged is a fortunate deed; it is fundamental to gain approval and support from the people.* A solid yang line supports and upholds the needy (the three broken yin lines above).

- **To receive:** *Gentle, appreciative, and properly centered people are more likely to receive good compensation. A person should remain honest and humble to impress the great leaders with the legitimate need for help.* Line two is a yin line in a yin position; it is centered and protected and is bonded with genuine loyalty to line two, the most powerful line, to distribute awards.

- *To ask for financial assistance:* One needs proof of merit, must be in a position to lead a needy group, and must be honest and sincere to properly dole out assistance. Above all, be honest about your needs and about what others can afford, and never ask for more than what you need or deserve. Line three is a yin line at the yang position and on the edge of the trigram, symbolizing a leader on the edge of a disaster.

- *To build good will:* When you move to a new territory, send gifts to your neighbors to establish your legitimate standing in the community. Line four is a yin line at the edge of the outer trigram, a new zone and a very shaky position; he needs support to stay centered in his new home.

- *When you reach a powerful position, use your position to benefit the people; your people will reward you with many happy returns.* A yang line properly sits in the highest position, in the right mind and with the power to do the right thing. He is bonded to line two, his subjects, getting support.

- *A powerful, greedy leader who burdens his subjects with excessive taxes or any unjustified taxes is inviting rebellion.* A yang line at the top is breaking through another yang barrier to press the yin lines for more support. The subjects ill bond to a great leader of lower rank to receive help and launch an attack.

Divination: The hexagram carries a good message on financial cooperation. You are likely to benefit from a good partnership. Credit your partner for the reward. Only a capable person can benefit from the message.

43 Kuai 夬
Parting

Kuai means "to separate, pull, or flow in different directions." Excessive or improper compensation drains the resources of the system. The five yang lines symbolize generous compensation, and the yin line on the highest position represents the breaking point.

The opening commentary reinforces the principle of giving: people performing good deeds to benefit others should not boast about their acts. They should give credit for all good things and blessings (including everything they own) to God.

While giving or doling out resources to the public (the needy), people have to watch out for misdeeds and corrupt people. This hexagram is about stopping improper compensation and fighting opponents.

Here is the procedure:

- *Get yourself fully prepared for the job. A small error will cost you a great fortune.* A yang line is in a yang position but is lowly and humble without enough force to complete the job. There is no bonding help

- *Stay alert to sudden attacks from the bad guys while you are doing your preparation.* A yang line is in a protected, centered position, but it is not secure, as this is not the right position.

- *Carefully conceal your motive from the bad guys while keeping your determination alive. Stay vigilant to avoid repercussions from your opponents.* Line three is at the edge, exposed to danger.

- *Move steadily to conceal your emotion while you are getting closer to your target.* Line four is in a new zone but is blocked by line five from reaching the crooked person; he is showing impatience. That will bring him misfortune.

- *While you have the power and position to destroy the bad guy, try to make him turn around to cooperate with your teammate before making a final decision.* A yin and a yang line are a natural pair, which offers the possibility for teamwork. However, success is not guaranteed; as the *I Ching* implies, there is always a change from the usual outcome.

- *The evil can never win over the good; they will be caught sooner or later.* We see one yin line against five yang lines at the dangerous edge of the outer zone. It eventually falls.

Divination: You are in a dilemma, searching for a quick and viable solution. The choice will not be easy and clear. Save your bait, and wait for the dust to clear.

44 Kou 姤
Encounter

```
━━━━━━━━━━━
━━━━━━━━━━━
━━━━━━━━━━━
━━━━━━━━━━━
━━━━━━━━━━━
━━━━━  ━━━━
```

Kou stands for unexpected encounters, new opportunities, or surprising provisions. When we try hard to do the right thing to the point of sacrifice, unexpected assistance can surface. The sacrifice will be noticed by the divine, who will reward our sacrifices.

These surprising opportunities or provisions could have many forms. Temptations abound. While we welcome new opportunities, we have to distance ourselves from undesirable temptations. Here are the procedures/laws on meeting new challenges:

- *Build a metal chain defense to resist the persistent approach of a new encounter.* A yin line at the yang position (someone with an unknown motive) is trying repeatedly to break through the yang barrier for a reason. Its improper position calls for precaution.

- *Add a defense net to keep the person on hold for evaluation before this person influences the environment.* Line two is a yang line in a yin position, not the right position for making a sound decision. He is in a critical protected zone to defend line four (his team member or boss) from falling into the trap of line one.

- *Refrain from reaching the new encounter when you are not close enough to observe properly or make a sound evaluation.* Line three is separated from line one by another yang line. He is also in an edge position, unprotected, and not centered, so he will not make a sound decision.

- *Blindly keeping a permanent distance from someone without making any effort to understand the person will incur the danger of missing opportunity. A leader staying away from his people will lose support from the people.* Line four is bonded to line one; the naturally bonded pair should get in contact somehow. There could be great opportunity in disguise.

- *When it comes to a point for action, the leader has to meet the encounter regardless of the potential danger. He has to exercise courage and prudence to score a victory. The new encounter could be beneficial.* Line five is a great leader in a right position, centered and protected. He has the capability to meet the challenge with prudence and to win.

- *Strip away the defense of your evil attacker with full force if necessary. For the safety of your kingdom, using your ruthlessness to conquer a foe is fully justified.* Line six is a yang line in yin position, combining physical and mental power to launch a good act.

Divination: *Kou* indicates a period of anxiety, challenges, or surprising rewards, normally involving a new romance. The strategy is not to force issues but to try your best and exercise great prudence. This hexagram favors June births.

45 Hsui 萃
Clustering

Hsui means "growing to abundance and achieving greatness." But obtaining good results takes effort. The fundamental trigrams are water in a pond and earth, representing irrigation of farmland. The scene in the four trigrams depicts a mother leading the young children; they are working together. A caring, loving leader unites the local folks for a community function, and all are of one mind and one heart.

Use the morals of fairness and integrity with some kindness. The elements in the scene are metal and earth, interbreeding and benefiting one another. This hexagram discusses the principles of gathering people to fulfill a goal.

Here are the laws:

- *Bravely and consistently fulfill your goals. Scream and yell to get help if you must.* Line one is humble, lowly, and in the wrong position; her bonding help is farther away, separated by two more yin lines. She needs to shout to line four for help until he responds. Getting help from the beginning is the *I Ching* way of succeeding.

- *Proceed with honesty, sincerity, and prudence. Your good hard work will be heard by the Almighty.* Line two is centered and protected (prudent and honest) but surrounded by yin lines (other evil people) on all fronts; she would succeed regardless of her difficult circumstances. Line five high above is bonded to her.

- *Gathering people for self-interest will not get you support.* Line three is a yin line in a wrong position (not in the right mind) and not bonded to any line, so she will not succeed.

- *If you have to use people of self-interest for some reason, you need to meet two conditions in order to succeed: (1) you must get support from above, and (2) you must get a good supporting base.* Line four, a yang, sits on a yin position of self-interest, but he sits next to the king and stays above three yin lines.

- *A benevolent, great leader will get good support from the people. If for some reason he is not winning their hearts from afar, he should consider performing more gracious good deeds.* Line five, a yang line in a right position, is centered and protected; he does the right thing and gets support. Though four yin lines support him, a deviant yang line waits below. He must be gracious when dealing with the negative situation.

- *If for some reason you are abandoned and betrayed by your people, repent and make a change.* Line six is a yin line separated from all other yin lines; the people are following other great leaders.

Divination: You may expect good fortune and wealth. However, hard and honest work is required. Eventually, you will need to distribute the goods wisely to maintain happiness.

46 *Sheng* 升
Progress

Sheng means "going up" or "advancing through effort." The two fundamental trigrams are wind and earth, representing the wind moving over the land. Among the four trigrams, the earth (the mother) is being supported by three children below; both the daughter and the son are grown, helping to take care of the very young and the mother. There is great progress in the family.

What are the rules of advancement?

- *Don't worry about a poor start. Follow the path of the gracious, great leaders. Learn from successful predecessors.* Line one is lowly, humble, and in the wrong position without bonding help. Such conditions, however, should not stop people from making progress.

- *Be determined, focused, flexible, and open-minded. You will eventually be rewarded with progress when you act with passion and honesty.* A yang line appears in a yin position but centered and protected. One does not need to be in the right position to move upward.

- *Move in continuous, steady steps. Take a step forward when circumstance allows.* Line three is a yang line in the right position, and three broken yin lines offer no resistance.

- *Keep moving upward on the right path; follow the proper procedure, and you will succeed.* Line four is a yin line in a yin position; it is not centered but is in the right mind and honest. One can make good progress with honest work regardless of position.

- *When you reach a high position, get good people to help you build up a secure jumping board and progress further.* A yin line is in a yang position but is not strong enough to keep the position. She should get help from line two.

- *Relentless upward movement without a base of support will create poor health and slow the pace. Practice self-control to preserve your energy for the long haul; the last five minutes are critical for the outcome.* Line six dangles from the top on a hollow base of two yin lines. Take precaution, and reevaluate your strategy.

Divination: Improvement, fulfillment of dreams, and accumulation of assets are in the picture. The fundamental trigrams depict the southeast and the southwest. All good things are happening in the south. You should focus on this direction when advancing.

47 Kun 困
Difficulty

Kun means "great difficulty and poverty." The two fundamental trigrams are the pond and the stream. Water from the pond (on the *Tui* trigram at the top of the hexagram) has become dry due to the steady leak to the stream (the *Kan* trigram) below.

The theme consists of two parts: (1) reasons to be trapped in poverty and (2) strategies for getting out of difficulty. Here are the laws:

- *Being docile and too lazy to make changes is unacceptable. Prolonged inactivity and staying in a destitute environment will put us in poverty without hope for recovery.* Line one is a yin line at the lowest and wrong position; its bonding help at line four is at the wrong position and unable to help.

- *Being frequently entertained by excessive food (extravagance or other excessive material comfort) will create odds for a sensible person, driving them out of good sense, possibly toward subsequent difficulty.* Line two is a yang line in a yin position flanked by vices/temptations on all fronts; it is without bonding help, a hazardous position leading to difficulty in life. It is in the wrong position and spoiled to inactive.

- *Being driven by ruthless greed (gambling) will eventually put people in difficulty, losing their job/home/family.* A yin line appears at the edge, taking improper and unnecessary risks. Blocked by two powerful yang lines on both ends, the person is going nowhere and must try to cope with the loss.

- *Relieving poverty is a slow and difficult process; it has to be well planned and effective.* Line four is bonded to and can rescue line one from poverty but is in a challenging position; he does have enough resources and is blocked by another yang line.

- *Physical, hard work and pain are good medicine; this encourages the individual to move to a higher level of accomplishment, while indulging in vices would corrupt him and put him into greater difficulty.* Line five, a yang in the right position, is centered and protected and sensible enough to do the right thing.

- *In extreme difficulty, search for proper options and get the right help.* Line six is a yin line at the right position and in the right mind to make correct decisions; being on the top, it is due to fall, a reversal of difficulty. There is no way to relieve poverty without seeking the proper options.

Divination: Expect dilemmas and uncertainty. Be patient, and face the problem with a positive attitude. This is a time for studying, sorting out options, and searching for solutions. Don't expect quick results.

48 *Ching* 井
The Well

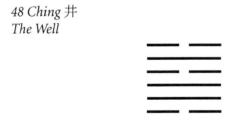

Ching is a well—the life water (for the people), the center of activity (for the community), and the root or source of conventional wisdom (to guide the people). A well is the technology, the wisdom, the link, and the source of livelihood for the people. It is public property and must be kept in clean, proper condition to benefit the people. Everyone has the obligation to maintain it in good working condition.

Keeping a well in good condition takes good people. The theme of this hexagram is recruiting good people to guide the livelihood of the community. For an individual, the lesson is on how to keep up with changes of time. A person's means of livelihood is like a well, to be kept up if you want to stay alive. Here are the scenarios on the wisdom of the well wisdom:

- *A dead well blocked with sand and mud does not provide water for the community. It is functionless.* If we don't move with time, we will share the fate of the dead well. Line one is on the bottom, a yin line not in the right position and broken (not holding crucial water).

- *A leaking bucket can't get water out of the well. We need the right tool (or means or skill) to get the precious water out. We need the right skill to make a living. The water below the well is also like good people trapped in obscurity; they need to be recruited with extra effort.* Line two is a yang line in a wrong position and not bonded by the king above, as both are yang. But line two deserves a chance.

- *Prepare a good procedure for recruiting good people. Clean up the sand to let the water out. It is the way to get good people out from the grass roots.* Line three is out of the well, like clean water picked up in a bucket and ready for use. We need to clear the path for good people to move upward.

- *Fix up the wall of the well. We should prepare ourselves for new opportunities.* Line four is a yin line between two yang lines (representing the wall being repaired), enjoying the bonding convenience nearby.

- *The emerging right people are like the clean, sparkling, gushing water from the new well; they should be assigned the right opportunities and use their full potential to serve the public.* Line five, the highest authority, sits on the right position, centered and protected, directing fair assignments.

- *The top official, upon receiving the assignment, should dedicate his or her service to all the people.* Line six, a yin line, is bonding to both yang lines at line five (close by and high) and at line three (a natural bonding mate) and serving all the people near and far.

Divination: Take part in community service. You could find hidden benefits. Just as a well serves water to the community, people are likely to be ready to help in return.

49 Ko 革
Revolution

Ko means "the skin of a cow" or the leather after the vigorous processing procedure. It implies thorough change or a revolution is coming, requiring sacrifice and force.

In the hexagram, the cow has been used as the chief animal to symbolize revolution in all commentaries. A cow is sturdy, hardworking, reliable, and productive. The two fundamental trigrams are *Tui* and *Li*, water and fire, conflicting elements, indicating two uncompromising scenarios. Big change is in order.

The most helpless grass-root citizens (three young women of different age ranks) are fed up with the corrupt leader and are trying to uproot the establishment (the father icon at the center, a mature male) from all fronts.

Here are the laws on revolution:

- *Revolution is risky; it has to be well planned.* Line one is a yang line without bonding support in the right position at the bottom of the society. He is unhappy about the corruption on the yin line above, but he knows to be patient and to make preparations.

- *Target the right time to raise the sentiment of anger among the people to get support; signs of big corruption and decay are good indicators of good timing.* Line two is a yin line in the right position, centered and protected, with bonding support. The time is right.

- *Think three times to make sure a revolution is necessary.* Line three is a yang line at the yang position, brave and in the right mind, with bonding help above, he is determined. However, he is at risk on the edge; he has to sort things out before entering the new zone.

- *Get support from the public.* Line four finally enters the revolution process; at the edge without bonding help, he apprehends the danger and begins to seek help from the people.

- *Make thorough changes down to the roots.* Line five has succeeded to overthrow the corrupt government. He is centered and protected. With great power, he bonds to the yin line above and to the yin line at line two, pushing changes in all parts of the country.

- *Match the new dynasty with a new outlook and new outfit, and rejoice with the people. The change should start with the leading class and quickly filter down to impact the lifestyle, attitude, and mentality of the people nationwide.* Line six, a yin line in the yin position and bonded to the yang lines below, is in the right mind to move the changes from line five down, one line a time.

Divination: You should go to the root of the problem and initiate a thorough change, uniting with the right people to make the change. When making decisions, you should choose the southeast direction for action. Avoid the northwest.

50 Ting 鼎
Vessel

A *ting* is a bronze cauldron with three feet and two ears, a sacred vessel used to cook food for sacrifice to gods and ancestors. It can be three things: (1) a cooking vessel used in the palace, (2) a decorative vessel for celebrations and ceremonies in the palace, and (3) a display of new a dynasty.

Cooking with high temperature changes the fundamental chemical or physical properties of materials; symbolically, cooking represents thorough change. Here are the procedures for implementing new laws:

- *Turn the vessel upside down and clean it thoroughly. That is, eliminate the stale residue, any nonfunctional system, from the old dynasty. Let the new people lead.* Line one is a broken line, flexible and open to change and cleaning. It stands at the front line, the beginning point for change.

- *Fill the vessel with good ingredients (good people), and detach it from all bad elements. Don't be concerned with how to position these good people; they will find their way and proper spots eventually.* Line two, a yang line in a yin position, removed from the old system below, is mingling with the other yang lines.

- *For the talented, capable individuals, the temporary setback of not serving in a good position should not deter them from polishing their skills for future opportunities.* Line three is on the edge (looking for opportunities from above) without bonding help and is waiting patiently for the position in line four, closer to the king.

- *When given the opportunity to serve, watch out for the evil guys. They should not be entrusted with important responsibilities.* Line four is finally next to the king. After naturally bonding to yin line one, he is tempted to offer favoritism to the incompetent. It would bring misfortune.

- *A capable individual needs the support of a great boss.* Line five is centered and protected and appreciates capable people, as depicted by the bonds with the yang lines up and down.

- *Mix people of complementary qualities and abilities to enhance the administration.* Line six, a yang, is bending to the yin at line five for help making decisions.

Divination: The time to prepare for a thorough change is now; it is a favorable time to kick an old, bad habit and turn over a new leaf. Getting on the right track is easier with help from the cosmos. The hexagram benefits the elder son.

51 Chen 震
Shake

Chen is great shock trembling like thunder. Dramatic change produces shock. *Chen* elaborates on how to handle shock. It is two trigrams of thunder, at times turning into water and sometimes blocked by a mountain (thick earth on land).

Shock is part of life. It is frightening, but it should not hurt well-prepared people. Evolved individuals learn to prepare for the outbreak.

There are no bonding pairs in the hexagram. Sudden shock is unpredictable, random, and often an isolated event; no one can count on bonding help. Handling shock is an individual challenge. How should someone respond to shock? Here are the laws:

- *Learn from the shock, and get ready for the next disaster. A well-learned lesson from the shock will create good fortune in the future. A wise person does not repeat a second mistake.* Line one is a yang line; the person is in his right mind, deciding to learn from his very first experience with shock and to apply the wisdom in future incidents (depicted by the other two unpredictable yin lines above).

- *Faced with an oncoming shock, stay calm and centered; escape to a safe place immediately, and forgo all your belongings because you will earn them back in the near future. Follow your prepared procedure; you will recover in seven days.* At the time of the *I Ching*, the shortest measuring unit for time was ten days. A seven-day period was shorter than this official time unit of time and was used to mean something would happen very soon. Line two sits at the center of a shock, a dangerous spot; however, being centered and prepared, she is not significantly harmed.

- *Taking an apprehensive attitude over shocks would keep us away from the shocks.* Line three at the edge of the trigram is unprotected and in constant fear of being hit by shocks. His apprehension earns him some protection from the yang line above.

- *Develop strength and power to meet the challenge of shocks. Otherwise, you will become the victim of shocks.* Line four is alone, at the wrong position, and surrounded by all yin (evil) forces; he is putting himself in a dangerous position.

- After *being hit by a shock, stay centered before making a move. Assess the cause of the shocking disaster; work on a remedy to stop the same thing from happening again in the future, or minimize its impact if it is impossible to avoid.* Line five, a yin in the wrong position, keeps a cool head; she will minimize the impact of the shock.

- *Your best defense to a shock is to stay alert in anticipation of its advancement and take precautions.* Line six is on the top, without bonding help or the support of a yang line; he should practice self-defense.

Divination: Adversity or difficulty will pass like a thunderstorm. The noise is temporary. Proceed with your plan. Work hard. Good things are coming your way.

52 *Ken* 艮
Stop

Ken means "to stop, limit, quiet, enclose, and mark off" or "to be adamant." A strong will is required to stop vices or to succeed against all odds.

The hexagram shows two mountain trigrams doubled up, signifying the strong determination needed to fulfill a goal or the total calmness required when facing a shock. Like the hexagram about shock, there are no bonding line pairs. Exercising willpower is a personal endeavor, a self-attained matter. There is no room for external help.

The theme of the hexagram is deterring temptations or vices. There are two forms of temptation. The first is greed; wise individuals should limit their desires within proper boundaries to remain sane. The second is the temptation to give up a set goal (or to stop your effort) upon encountering obstacles.

Here is the strategy for staying on track:

- *Put your willpower to work at the very beginning when you try to stop something. It prevents errors from cropping up.* Line one, a yin in a yang position, is prone to commit errors.

- *Failing to stop an error when you need to will make you very unhappy.* Line two—correctly positioned, centered, and sensible—is working hard for a solution against some poor odds. She has to serve the yang line immediately above, which is not her right bonding partner; she is unhappy with the incompatible mate.

- *Failing to get out of the battlefield between two forces on two sides will make you a loser, a great misfortune.* Line three, unprotected at the edge of the territory, is caught between four yin lines, two on each side. Both sides are hostile toward each other. He is brutalized by both, becoming a victim.

- *Practicing self-discipline to stop a vice or bad mistake at the proper time will bring you good fortune.* Line four, a yin line in a yin position, knows how to exercise self-control and frees herself from the bond.

- *Use effective language to stop the bad mistake from happening.* Line five is centered and protected. She knows how to stop misfortune from happening. The power of words is stronger than a sword.

- *Hang on to the end, to the highest goal of self attainment.* Line six is a yang line on the highest level, sturdily overlooking the yin lines.

Divination: Advancement is not favored. When making decisions or choosing options, wise people will look to the mountains and the northeast for their actions. These places offer better rewards and opportunities. Avoid enterprises with water. Good fortune will arrive with strong will. Look to highlands or mountains for good fortune.

53 Chien 漸
Infiltration

The theme of the hexagram is adjusting to a new environment, partnership, or job. A wood trigram appears above the mountain, representing trees and plants slowly coming out of the mountain. Vegetation needs irrigation; success requires continuous effort and patience.

The trigrams depict, four children of different ranks growing up together, a gradual process. The scenario is wind slowly emerging from the mountain into the open space. *Chien* calls for slow and gradual moves when implementing corrections.

The hexagram uses the analogy of "preparing the wedding of a daughter" to illustrate the procedure. It is a deliberately cautious procedure of finding the right groom, observing propriety (the proper ceremony), and implementing the arrangements to unite the couple.

Here is the procedure:

- *Go slowly at the beginning. Do not force issues; gradually move according to your strength.* Line one is a humble yin line in the wrong position (and not in the right mind) without bonding help from above; she can only succeed with slow steps.

- *Gradually seek help to build a rock-solid foundation as you advance. All parties involved in the act have to be in proper agreement to reach a common goal. Otherwise, there will be misfortune. A couple that is not in love will not produce good children.* Line two is centered and protected with bonding help from line five, a fortunate stage.

- *Watch your steps as you move. Don't go too far too fast as to alienate your support in the family. You could end up a loser, forfeiting all your gains.* Line three, a brave and reckless yang line, moves to the edge away from her support. She unwittingly settles in a bad relationship with line four nearby for convenience. She is forsaken by her family.

- *On your forward-moving path, take a submissive role to gain support when you fall into an uncomfortable scenario. Stay flexible and open-minded while advancing. Good fortune will come upon those who stay centered.* Line four is a yin line in the right position (in the right mind to do the right thing); she is gaining support from line five above and from line three below.

- *Have the courage to hold tight to your standing on whatever progress you have achieved. You will eventually conquer the obstacles to and reach your destination.* Line five has reached the highest point on her upward path. However, she is temporarily blocked by lines three and four from bonding to her natural partner at line two. The outcome will be fortunate, eventually.

- *The super human might reach a point where nothing will matter to him. If for some reason you fail to succeed in the world, do not bend to evil; keep doing what you must. Your spirit will inspire other followers to do good deeds* Line six is a yang line bonding to no one and stays solid and high, representing the ultimate goal for extraordinary men and women.

Divination: This hexagram gives procedures to the female for improving her marriage. Others can expect good fortune to come their way after a difficult beginning.

54 Kuei Mei 歸妹
Wedding

Kuei Mei in Chinese means "marrying your younger sister to someone," usually as a second wife.

The two fundamental trigrams of this hexagram are the first son and the third daughter, with a large age gap symbolizing unequal rank or incompatible status. The marriage is awkward. For the bride, the union is not honorable or desirable, but it is her only option for survival.

As the trigrams show, the female takes the lead in the search for partnership; she does it for her own livelihood. The theme illustrates the attitudes for evaluating unpleasant options in our life paths at given points in time. It also refers to moonlighting.

The *I Ching* realizes that many of us have to take inferior or/disgraceful jobs to tide over some difficult time. Managing such a situation takes special wisdom.

Here are the rules to play by:

- *Take the odd honest job (as a second wife, in lower rank, of course), or an inferior but morally legitimate job, to make a living, and do your best to perform your role properly. Good fortune will follow.* Line one is a yang line in the right position, meek but sturdy and hardworking. There is no bonding help. The person needs to earn a living on his or her own.

- *Respect and serve your superior (your husband, the first wife, the boss, your provider, etc.) with loyalty and respect even though he or she does not measure up to the position or the inferior job title does not measure up to your capacity.* Line two is a capable person (a yang line) in a low, improper yin position (meaning this person has not met the right boss or found the right job). The superior, a yin line, sits in a higher position with unfit ability. Regardless of the uncomfortable circumstance, line two naturally bonds to his boss and shows loyalty. This act will bring good fortune in the future.

- *You need to develop solid credentials to qualify for a good position.* Line three, a yin line with limited ability, moves upward to take chances; she will not succeed, as she is not prepared for good jobs. There is no bonding line above, and she is not centered or protected.

- *Regardless of hardship, take time to line up an honest job (or to marry an honest person), and you will eventually build your career.* Line four, a yang line in a yin position, has remained single (or unemployed) for a long time. A yin line nearby is ready to pair up with her; they are not proper partners, but the union is convenient. Seriously consider such options.

- *Focus on your inner strength, and maximize your qualifications to meet the demands of the job market. Superficial outfits stand as secondary.* Line five, the princess of the emperor, can easily attract great suitors;

she does not need shiny outfits. All three yang lines will be attracted by her glamorous status and make generous offers.

- *Vanity and lack of substance will bring fruitless results.* Line six, a vain and dishonest yin line, waits in a dangerous and shaky position.

Divination: If you have this hexagram in your life cycle, you could be in some difficulty and having a hard time achieving a goal. Don't expect a perfect solution. On the other hand, the hexagram could also indicate the possibility of moonlighting for a second income.

55 Feng 豐
Abundance

Feng means "abundance." Resources grow as a result of gradual advancement and new sources of income. However, the success is too brilliant, like a midday sun that has begun its gradual decline.

The two fundamental trigrams are the *Chen* and the *Li*, representing the bright sun in the spring, loud and bright; all four trigrams are young people in their prime vibrancy. As the laws of change dictate, what has reached the zenith has to go down. No abundance stays forever. The theme of the hexagram is about handling abundance:

- *Pursuing abundance is our birthright; the key is to determine the right kind and the right amount of abundance within the proper course. When we pursue it over the limit, it creates misfortune.* Line one is a yang line in a correct position (symbolizing a capable young man in his right mind to pursue a goal). Without bonding help, he has to search alone.

- *Look for connections to help when pursuing abundance. While solid help is hard to find, search diligently for options.* Line two is centered and protected but facing challenges. Her natural help at line five is a yin line of low ability, but they do not bond. Her other option is to coach her partner above to produce mutually beneficial abundance.

- *The path to abundance is hazardous and full of hassles. Avoid being ruthless so that you don't get permanent injuries along your path.* Line three is at the zenith of the sun's path (the last line of the *Li* trigram), the point of decline. He could recoup and start over by seeking help from line six, provided he could regain his capacity to fight. The road to abundance is never smooth.

- *Network with the right helpers below when you are not in the position to receive support from a good superior.* Line four, a yang line (capable and strong), sits in a yin position below a yin line (with no strength); he should join with the two likeminded yang lines below to launch a successful venture.

- *As a feeble leader sitting on a high position, you can achieve abundance by calling in all the able-bodied good people from afar to help.* Line five, a yin line, is at the king position with another yin line above. Her rescuers are the three yang lines below.

- *Avoid, by all means, being cornered in isolation upon success. Reach out and share with others to avoid self-destruction.* Line six, a yin line next to another yin, is isolated, a dangerous scenario.

Divination: Prepare for declining fortune; have plans for a rebound. Good times for achieving abundance are in the spring—particularly during the rabbit, tiger, and dragon years, months, or days, depending on the timeframe of your projects. Heed the warning to limit advances.

56 Lu 旅
Sojourning

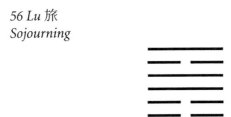

Lu means "travel" or "staying in a temporary home." It can also mean the need to migrate to a new location in pursuit of abundance. The scene depicts the sun and the wind trapped in the mountain, indicating unpleasant situations and barriers. Yang and yin lines are interspersed in equal number with only one pair of corresponding lines, symbolizing an unsteady mood and the need to balance emotion. Here are the rules in this hexagram:

- *Pack only crucial essentials; preserve resources to handle survival issues. Bottom line—travel light!* Line one is yin line at the wrong position; her bonding help is attracted to another yin line above. She needs to take precautions when facing these odds.

- *Carry sufficient funds, and bring good people with you.* Line two is in the right position, centered and protected, but she can't count on bonding help from afar. She needs to be well prepared.

- *Be good to your help, and spread good will to your new neighbors.* Line three is away from the protected position and is about to enter a new territory. With no prospects for bonding help from afar, he needs to find support nearby.

- *Do not expect to feel at home in a new environment; make yourself comfortable as much as possible.* Line four is already settled in a new land and looks back to line one for support, as he is homesick. He should try to bond to line five, another yin line.

- *Continue to try hard to adapt to the new home by being open, honest, and generous with your new neighbors; you will eventually establish yourself and reach the top.* Line five is a yin line at the wrong position, but she is strong enough to fulfill her goal. She tries to bond to the yang line above.

- *A rebellious attitude will lead to misfortune.* Line six, a yang line, is in a wrong and risky position at the top without bonding help.

Divination: Pay attention to what you do and say. Take good care of financial matters. Be generous with small gifts. Expect a period of uncertainty.

57 Sun 巽
Taking a Shelter

Sun in Chinese means "obeying and accommodating." The hexagram is about the proper attitudes for followers of a great leader or a provider.

There are two *Sun* trigrams (the wind and the first daughter) to reinforce the nature of wind blowing into every crack and little hole; it symbolizes a flexible individual following every helpful lead and taking every small opportunity for support.

There are more yang lines, emphasizing the importance of honesty. Yang lines outside show strength and confidence, and yin lines inside indicate caution.

Here are the rules on seeking support:

- *Be determined, courageous, and committed to following a good supporter. Hesitation will lead you nowhere.* Line one is a yin line at a yang position, low and uncomfortable, without help from above. It is trying to bond to the two yang lines above.

- *Don't feel humiliated when you have to bow and kneel to show total respect to a provider/supporter. Keep your self-confidence and morale up.* Line two, youthful and strong, chooses (because he is centered and in his right mind) to bend to a humble, lowly position, looking for provisions and guidance from the line above.

- *Obey your provider/supporter sincerely. Dishonesty backfires eventually.* Line three, under a humble disguise, is secretly inching upward to an unprotected zone, trying to rebel and sneak into another shelter. But there is no bonding help (line four, as a yin, does not bond to line three). It is, therefore, very hazardous.

- *Serve your provider/supporter properly, sincerely contributing your best to benefit your provider; you will be abundantly rewarded.* Line four, a yin line, sits in a yin position, humbly and properly serving the boss above.

- *Use prudence to perform a loyal, supporting role to your provider. Plan ahead, and evaluate the results afterward.* Line five is at the highest position, properly centered and protected. He is capable of using prudence to perform his supporting role. Don't take things for granted. Earn your provisions.

- *Change your attitude and course to lead a new life as soon as you are established in your position. Modesty is not forever. Excessive modesty from a highly capable individual creates misfortune.* Line six is on top without a bonding line; as a yang line, he chooses to hide on a yin (obscure) position. He is isolating himself and inviting misfortune.

Divination: You are a dependent. You need to be a good guest by being gentle, flexible, honest, and soothing like the wind. Eventually, you will resolve your dilemma. Meanwhile, don't expect to achieve a big goal or to receive a big reward. Rewards will come later.

58 Tui 兑
The Pursuit of Joy

This hexagram is discussed in the text.

Divination: The hexagram benefits the teaching, coaching, and consulting professions. The favorable time is the fall, during evenings with full moons; look to the west for direction.

59 Huan 渙
Dispersal

Huan means "dispersion" or "disintegration." *Huan* describes obstacles, illusions, and misunderstandings. It emphasizes the natural process of clearing obstacles and taking a natural course when tiding over an unpleasant situation.

The two fundamental trigrams are the *Sun* and the *Kan* (wind and water, wood and river, ocean); they could symbolize a boat on the river or ocean heading to a far-away land.

The theme of the hexagram's lines, in fact, is preventing a dispersing crowd or mob from gaining momentum:

- *Take action at the first sight of a dispersing crowd. Use a powerful horse to round up the dispersing crowd and restore the order.* Line one is a yin line in a wrong position; the crowd needs a good leader.

- *Provide a stool (a shelter) for everybody in the crowd to keep them in place.* Line two, a yang line in an improper yin position, is centered and secure. This person should make the minimum arrangements to keep the crowd together.

- *Avoid self-interest, and practice fair play with everybody.* Line three sits at the edge in a yang position. The person is trying hard to be open and fair.

- *Reach out to people from all fronts.* Line four is at the right position, in the right mind, and wise enough to do the right thing. As a yin line at the highest position, she has the power to bond to any yang line; because none of the yang lines is her natural mate, she has no favorite.

- *Send a clear signal, and distribute governmental resources to put the disorganized people together.* Line five is centered, protected, and in the highest position to give commands. He has no bonding line. He can treat everyone equally.

- *Stay away from the disturbed crowd to avoid bloodshed if the crowd falls out of control.* Line six is away from the crowd in line one and should not bond to any line.

Divination: You are likely to experience some great challenges, but they will eventually go away without causing damage. Traveling afar to pursue your dreams should be rewarding. Staying close to home will lessen your chance of success.

60 Chieh 節
Articulating

Chieh in Chinese means "the divider between the sections of a bamboo stalk." It blocks and divides in a set order. Therefore, it also means controlling vices and harmful desires. The bottom line is discipline.

The two fundamental trigrams are water and pond, depicting flowing water held up by a pond. All four trigrams are the youngest members in the society, and they need guidance. All lines are in two equal groups: three yang and three yin. One group has one yang and one yin, while the other group has two yang and two yin, showing the magnitude and order of control.

Here are the laws:

- *Discipline starts with self-control of desires and vices.* Line one is yang line in the right position. He bonds to the yin line four but is blocked by another yang line right above. He patiently keeps himself in place, as the time is not right for any movement.

- *Move at the right time. Excessive hesitation would create misfortune.* Line two has advanced in position, becoming close enough to bond with line three or line four and to move upward. The time is right to gain. However, he hesitates, as he worries about the disapproval from line five, a yang line. The hesitation will result in misfortune.

- *Losing self-control will cost you dearly.* Line three should stay in a lower position, but she is tempted to advance to an improper position at the wrong time. She lingers unprotected at the edge without bonding help because she has nowhere to turn.

- *Proper self-control will win you approval from above.* Line four is at the right position, centered and bonded to line five. She exercises proper control and is protected from errors. She, therefore, gets support from her superior.

- *Discipline inspired by a role model from the top should be the most effective.* Line five is a yang line at the right position, leading the people.

- *Extreme control and discipline induce pain. They don't work.* Line six, a yin line conforming to the right position and creeping upward, is trying to exercise extreme self-control.

Divination: You are advised to exercise self-control and moderation, keeping possessions to a minimum. The favorable direction for action is the west.

61 Chung Fu 中孚
Integrity

Chung means "conforming, centered, sincere, truthful, or reliable." *Fu* means "giving birth after proper pregnancy." Because the arrival of a newborn provides good evidence of the initial date of a woman's (or an animal's) pregnancy, *Fu* refers to proven trust by evidences.

The virtues included in the trigrams are fairness, kindness, and integrity. There is symmetry in the lines: two yin lines are flanked by two yang lines (double, solid honesty), a perfectly conforming order. Lines two and five, the key team, have no bonding mates; they are absolutely independent and objective. *Chung Fu*, therefore, symbolizes a clear order of honesty.

The layout resembles a flying bird steadily measuring the altitude for a safe landing by searching for reliable signs (or evidence). That is, trust is built on hard evidence. The theme of the hexagram is evaluating integrity.

Here are the principles:

- *Carefully evaluate the integrity of your associates; close relatives/friends are not necessarily trustworthy. An error could be costly; changing course could cause misfortune.* Line one is a yang line in the right position and bonded to line four. He sees things in the proper perspective and does not count on the loyalty of line four. Line four could change course to bond to line five above or to gang up with the bad influence (line three, which is not in a correct position) below.

- *To evaluate integrity, we need to put the following into perspectives: (1) their words and acts and (2) their public and private behaviors. We can trust someone if his words match his deeds in both private and public life.* Line two is centered and protected but in a wrong position and has no bonding line. He has to prove himself with good deeds.

- *A change of course to adjust your error in judgment would upset your plan. Be calm and consistent to show your integrity. Showing your emotion would not get you good results.* Line three naturally bonds with line six, but he inches ahead to compete with line four for the job from the boss in line five. That creates an emotional fight with line four.

- *Gain the trust of a great leader.* Line four bonds naturally to line one; however, she abandons line one and bonds to line five above.

- *Practice integrity only toward deserving people who can help you in return. Integrity creates great fortune when both parties highly value it. With the wrong people, misfortune occurs.* Line five, a yang correctly at the highest-ranking position, is pairing up with line two; both are yang (having great integrity) and centered.

- *Put your integrity in the right or in good services; never isolate yourself with rigid principles that are hard to practice. Setting yourself apart with excessive and extreme integrity will put you in a shaky, isolated spot. A rooster rigidly reports the right time to the universal public and always stays grounded; it can never fly high.* Line six, a yang line at the yin position, is prevented by line five from connecting to other lines. The person is doing the wrong thing in an isolated spot. "Honesty is the best policy," but only when it is practiced at the right place, toward the right people, and at the right time. Change is the rule of the game.

Divination: To succeed, you must be honest. The line structure of the hexagram resembles a boat (hollow inside with yin lines, balanced and elevated at both ends by yang lines). You will ride along with the wind on top of a pond. It is a favorable time for seeking fortune in a foreign land.

62 Hsiao Kuo 小過
Over Limit

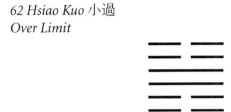

Hsiao means "small." *Kuo* means "crossing." Together, *Hsiao Kuo* means "taking a small step over the limit to make a difference." The theme is on deviating properly from the norm to achieve a better result without violating the code.

Two yang lines inside represent strong desire, and four yin lines outside the trigrams busily experiment with different little schemes to fulfill the goal. The two yang lines also symbolize the body of the bird, while the yin lines on both sides represent the flapping wings; the bird is testing the altitude before taking off.

How does one proceed?

- *Match your expectations with your capacity. Trying to fly high without the assistance of good winds is a misfortune.* Line one is trying to move upward to bond to its natural mate at line four; however, as a yin line in the yang position, it does not have the right conditions for success.

- *Take any available help, and make the best of it. Settle for the second best when necessary.* Line two is centered and protected and in her right mind to do the right thing; her bonding help at line five happens to be yin (of lesser help) instead of yang, as it should be, but she happily accepts the odds.

- *Be flexible to forgo the small gains in hazardous situations.* Line three has moved to a risky zone, trying to bond with line six for some advancement. Unfortunately, line six has bad company (two bonded yin lines); line three, a yang line in the right position, should avoid associating with line six.

- *A little courtesy goes a long way. Do not bluntly reject an associate for improper favors. This is for your protection.* Line four is a yang line bonding to the yin at line one; he is approached by a dishonest person asking for favors. He gently uses yin tactics for protection.

- *Settle with small gains when your strength is limited. Do not insist on your entitlements.* Line five, on a high and kingly position, has unrealistic expectations. However, as a feeble yin line without proper help (line two is also yin), she does not have enough power to lay claim to her entitlements.

- *Unlimited greed or gain will push a person into a danger zone. A bird flying beyond its comfort zone will expose itself to the arrows.* Line six has reached the highest point of no return, is unable to get support from its weak neighbor, and is blocked by yang line four from reaching his bonding help on line three.

Divination: You should try to tie up the loose ends of all small matters at hand, looking for small gains and patiently waiting for a good time to achieve an important goal. Play modestly. The horse and rat years, months, or days are good times to take little chances.

63 *Chi Chi* 既濟
Success

Chi Chi is "to complete" or "to succeed." The theme of the hexagram is handling and holding onto success. "While achieving success is hard, holding onto it is even harder," warns an old Chinese saying.

Here are the rules:

- *Thoroughly explore all potential pitfalls that could erode your success, and take precautions.* Line one is a yang line in the right position, bonded to line four, which is yin and in the right position as well (i.e., using the right judgment).

- *Success is about taking the right opportunity; evaluate potential opportunities carefully. Don't worry about losing one or two opportunities; better ones will come along soon.* Line two is a yin line at the yin position, protected on both sides, and open to opportunities on all fronts.

- *Preserve your energy for the worthy opportunity. When you win the battle, reward all your helpers in different ways (with money or a good job), but reserve the posts (jobs) to the good and trustworthy people only.* Line three is yang line at the right position; he has won the battle and is gaining respect from the yin lines.

- *Take elaborate precautions to protect your successes and gains.* Line four, a yin line at a yin position, is at the edge of a big river. She has to carefully prepare the boat for the crossing.

- *As you reach the zenith of your success, remind yourself of the simple life and high spirit in the old days when you started on your career path. Never stay complacent. Pride comes before a fall.* Line five is a yang line in the yang position at the high spot, enjoying great success. However, the high ground is surrounded by water waiting for his downfall.

- *Refrain from advancing into the deep water. Learn from the lesson of a greedy fox that drowned in the water. Don't let your desire to succeed confuse your steps.* Line six is a yin line in the yin position near the rolling water; she is in the right mind to understand the danger of drowning.

Divination: Stay alert to keep up with the good work. Exercise wisdom and courtesy when moving forward, and keep water and fire (conflicting elements) in perfect balance.

64 Wei Chi 未濟
Experimenting

```
━━━━━  ━━━━━
━━━━━━━━━━━
━━━━━  ━━━━━
━━━━━━━━━━━
━━━━━  ━━━━━
━━━━━━━━━━━
```

The two Chinese characters carry different meanings. *Wei* means "incomplete and temporal." *Chi* is "to successfully cross a river at a shallow spot." The moral is to experiment!

None of the lines is in the proper position; all yang lines are in yin positions, and all yin lines are in yang positions. Although the lines are in teams, their awkward positions prevent them from connecting. These are the typical characteristics of experiments. You have the right hypothesis (you are connected), but you need to properly prove it.

The theme of the hexagram is verifying ideas. Here is the procedure:

- *Go slow. A hasty action or erroneous conclusion will lead to disgrace. It is like a fox trying to cross a river in haste, without sufficient knowledge of the water; it drowned as a result.* Line one is a yin line in a yang position trying to get to the other side of the water; it is blocked by the yang line two. Take the barrier as a warning sign.

- *Exercise self-control to stay centered. Do not make assumptions.* Line two is a yang line in a yin position but centered, trying to stay above the water before going to either side. He is aware that he is not at the right spot, but he is brave and smart enough to stay objective.

- *Be brave to go after your points at the key moment. That is, when you are convinced of the validity of your discovery, take the risk to go against the public myth (passing the dangerous torrents of the river).* Line three, a yin line in a yang position at the edge of his home front, is getting ready to cross a new frontier.

- *Mobilize all your courage and resources to support your point if you have to, regardless of fierce counterpoints from the public.* Line four is a yang line (a courageous person) in a wrong position in a new territory; establishing his point will be a tough task. He needs patience and to perform great mental work to succeed.

- *Gather all good believers and supporters to work together.* Line five has reached a high position and is gaining recognition. As a yin line, he does not have enough power to implement his argument. Fortunately, he is centered enough to gather good help from all fronts.

- *After all the hard work, relax and leave the outcome to God. No one can force an issue against the Lord.* Line six is at a risky position on the wrong line without proper help; he is facing many odds. However, as a yang line on a yin position, he stays calm with great courage.

Divination: It is not a good time to expect results. You should keep trying and remain in good spirits during your journey.

Topics in the
Sixty-Four Hexagrams

1.	Chien, Yang Force	The great leader,
2.	Kun, Yin Force,	The assistant
3.	Chun, Sprouting_6	Starting a career
4.	Mung, Learning_7	Teaching and learning
5.	Hsu, Peer Competition	Competing with peers
6.	Sung, Litigation	Handling litigation
7.	Shih, Warring_4	Conducting a war
8.	Pi, Teamwork_4	Leading an organization
9.	Hsiao Chu, Small Saving	Gaining with small capital
10.	Lu, Propriety	Rules on advancing in position
11.	Tai, Prosperity_4	Wealth building
12.	PI, Obstruction	Correcting social inequality
13.	Tung Jen, Fellowship_4	Leading with charisma
14.	Tai Yu, Great Possession_4	Leading by talent
15.	Chien, Open-mindeness	Practicing modesty
16.	Yu, Provisions	Handling good fortune.
17.	Sui, Immigration	Adjusting to a new society
18.	Kui, Decay	Correcting corruption from predecessors
19.	Lin, New Leadership	Building a new leadership
20.	Kuan, Good Example	Educating the people by signs
21.	Shib Ho, Punishment	Applying punishments
22.	Pi, Civil Grace	Practicing ceremonies
23.	Po, Exfoliation	Stopping a decaying process
24.	Fu, Recovery	Making a recovery
25.	Wu Wang, Follow the Reality	A message on the truth
26.	Ta Chu, Great Accumulation	Getting power to achieve a goal
27.	Yi, Nourishment_6	Taking nourishment/finding provision
28.	Tai Kuo, Great Crossing_7	Pursuing a big dream
29.	Kan, Danger	Handling deep trouble

30. Li, Radiance_6	Being a transient dependent
31. Hsien, Dating_5	Rules on the dating game
32. Heng, Marriage_5	Managing a marriage
33. Tun, Retreat	Retreating from danger
34. Ta Chuang, Expansion	Making a comeback
35. Chin, Advancing	Seeking approval from a boss
36. Ming I, Getting Hurt	Avoiding an attack
37. Chia Jen, Family_5	Managing a family
38. Kuie, Polarizing	Handling difference and contrarians
39. Chien, Limping,_6	Being trapped in difficulty
40. Hsieh, Releasing	Solving a problem
41. Sun, Sacrifice	Taxing the people
42. Yi, Benefit	Give-and-take
43. Kuai, Parting	Stopping improper compensation
44. Kou, Encounter	Handling new opportunities
45. Hsui, Clustering	Gathering people to fulfill a goal
46. Sheng, Progress	Increasing assets
47. Kun, Difficulty	Managing difficulty
48. Ching, The Well	Recruiting good people
49. Ko, Revolution	Laws on revolution
50. Ting, Vessel	Implementing new laws
51. Chien, Shake	Shock management
52. Ken, Stop	Resisting temptation/vices
53. Chien, Infiltration	Implementing a slow correction
54. Kuei Mei, Wedding	Taking an inferior job
55. Feng, Abundance	Handling abundance
56. Lu, Sojourning	Handling a trip
57. Sun, Taking a Shelter	Following a great leader
58. Tui, Joy_7	Pursuing joy
59. Huan, Dispersal	Handling a dispersing crowd
60. Chieh, Articulating	Self-control
61. Chung Fu, Integrity	Handling integrity
62. Hsiao Kuo, Over Limit	Going over the limit
63. Chi Chi, Success	Handling success
64. Wei Chi, Experimenting	Conducting Research

Note: The fifteen hexagrams that are discussed in the text have a chapter number attached to the end of the hexagram.

References

1. Browne, Dennis. "The Source of All Power for Real Life Wizards"—The Cosmic Energy Web., http://www.dantewilson.com/cosmic energy.htm

2. Chung, Lily. *The Path to Good Fortune: The Meng.* St. Paul, MN: Llewellyn, 1997.

3. Chung, Lily. *Easy Ways to Harmony.* [San Francisco, City], CA: Gold Medal Book, 1999.

4. Donovan, Doug. "Poor me. I'm Rich" articles in Forbes, April 5, 1999.

5. Durant, Will. *The Story of Philosophy, 2ⁿᵈ Edition* (the lives and opinions of the world's greatest philosophers from Plato to John Dewey) Washington Square Press, 1953.

6. Hatch, Robert. "Newton, Isaac." *Encyclopedia Americana.*

7. Flint, Jerry. "A Vintage Contrarian", article in Forbes, November 16, 1998

8. McGreal, Ian P. *Great Thinkers of the Eastern World.* [New York, NY]: Harper Collins, 1995.

9. "The Life of Thomas Edison," article in Wikipedia, the free encyclopedia, 2001.

10. "The Pursuit of Happiness", collection of articles from contemporary celebrities on the subject. The ASAP EDITION, Forbes, Winter, 2001.

11. Wing, R. L. *The Tao of Power (Lao Tzu's Classic Guide to Leadership, Influence, and Excellence).* [Garden City, NY]: Dolphin Book/Doubleday & Company, Inc., 1986.

12. 余春台編、窮通寶鑑 (How cosmic flows Impact human lives)、新光出版社、香港. 九龍.

13. 孫振聲，白話易經 (The I Ching in Modern language), 星光出版社，澳門，中國，1987.

14. 邵康節與陳搏，河洛理數 (The I Ching Divination of Kan-Tze Shaw) 星星出版社，香港. (The book was first written in the Sung dynasty, reprinted in some editions in the format of modern time, printing time of this copy is unavailable.)